In gratitude to the mystery and to the game of life

A Lionhearted Bear publication

ISBN: 978-0-9571642-5-3

Paperback edition first published in 2015 by R.A. Moseley. This second revised edition first published in 2018.

This paperback has been produced by Create Space.

'The kingdom of God cometh not with observation; neither shall they say, Lo here! or, Lo there!, for behold, the kingdom of God is within you.'

Luke (xvii. 20, 21)

Author's Preface

After having conceived the idea of writing this book a few years ago, I recently discovered in my research, not unsurprisingly perhaps, that I was not alone in perceiving the deeper mystery and teachings contained in the game of golf; and the invitation of life changing transformation that it offers for the willing soul who plays it. Michael Murphy's book Golf in the Kingdom, first published in 1972, was one that stuck out noticeably. In reading it I had to ask myself whether there was anything new to add to his work.

Murphy's book came right at the beginning of a quiet revolution in western culture that has been taking place over the past fifty years. It is not a revolution you hear mentioned in the newspapers but beneath the radar, when you look closely, you will see there has been a gathering momentum in the quest for more awakened states of both human and global consciousness.

His story provides a tale of fiery initiation into such a state of consciousness; which he experienced when playing the legendary Burningbush golf course in Scotland in 1956 with an enlightened Master. His game tells a tale of transformation that was neatly split into two halves (he records that he was able to reduce his score on the second half of the course by a remarkable eighteen shots). From this fiery initiation he spent an evening in the company of souls who gave him a glimpse of the substance that lay beyond what he had experienced. The Master then took him back to the course in the middle of the night and took him deeper and deeper into the mystery.

But as Murphy himself writes; what he tasted was only a glimpse that was supported by some notes he copied from the Master's journal in the light of the following morning. These experiences, and the notes in his journal, offer a tantalising taste of the Master's teaching; but there is not enough here to get ourselves stuck in and rooted down by it. The fiery experience of the mystery rips apart and shreds away the illusory world that we had always thought was solid and real...but it doesn't help us to rebuild the new earth from the ashes left behind.

Shivas Irons, the Master who took Murphy into the fire, is very much like the Jesus of Nazareth that I see portrayed in the Gospel of Mark. Enigmatic to the core; he is the one who has been swept up by the mystery and is destined to remain misunderstood except for the few insiders who fully grasp his teaching. He is the archetypal stranger and it seems significant that Shivas was not your typical golfing professional who works within the confines of the golf club he is employed by. He is an outsider who hides in the shadows and who teaches the game of golf in his own way. And like Jesus, Shivas then vanishes into thin air and his teaching becomes the story of myth rather than reality. Did he really exist is the one unanswered question that all of us are left with from Murphy's tale.

Though Murphy recognised the Master, he himself admits that he had to scarper from him before he'd fully grasped the teaching. He had to leave because in truth it takes time for us to catch up and to integrate what has been received through the fiery initiation process. Murphy clearly needed time out to absorb and digest lest he become annihilated by spending too much time in the Master's powerful presence. Caroline Myss is one modern day mystic who reminds us that we have to go away and do the work of developing a soul with stamina before we can root ourselves that close to the fire. How interesting it is then that the mystical experience seduces us in and scares us away in equal measure. In truth it scares us because when the moment happens it possesses the power to blow the self right out of the control tower at the centre of our lives. The Burningbush is truly not a place for meddling by the weak of heart.

The number seven appears significant here in his story for it was around 1963, seven years after he left Scotland, that Murphy was ready to get back in touch with the Master (but co-incidentally it appears as if this was the same year that Shivas Irons left Scotland behind). It was then another seven years before Murphy was ready to return to Scotland and to continue on with his own journey. Interestingly, as I begin to write this book, we are marking the beginning of the seventh, seven year cycle since this return trip was taken.

Having fled from the Master, what Murphy leaves us with then are many tantalising and uncompleted threads, and he encourages those of us who recognise the mystery to help weave these together. In response to his plea the Shivas Irons society was formed some twenty years after his book was first published (and which co-incidentally was the same year that I began my own love affair with the game).

Now a further twenty years on, it is my view that, after half a century of exposure to this New Age, those of us living in the western world are better placed to go deeper and further along the path in order to grasp more fully the set of mystical teachings that this game has to offer.

The following story is based on my own experiences from the game of golf. But let it be said upfront that whilst I've been playing golf for a long time now, I do not claim to hold any mastery over my little white ball and I am nothing more than a mid-range handicapper who has had a few lucid moments of magic sprinkled upon me over the years. I am no expert and these writings are not designed to teach you the ways to become a better golfer.

My lack of expertise doesn't daunt me though because as the Buddha famously noted; it is critically important not to confuse the raft for the other shore. The fascination that has led to these writings comes only from the discovery that the game of golf has been nothing more and nothing less than a suitable vehicle for taking the bigger soul journey at hand...and is not to be confused as a destination in itself.

So the one essential question I am grappling with in these writings is; how can the time I spend on the golf course help to animate my soul so that I may go forth and live a more congruent life in this world?

Once it was only in monasteries that a rare few individuals would be called to engage with these deep questions of inquiry. But ever since the spiritual explosion of the 1960s, an increasing number of us in the western world today find ourselves being called to address these questions whilst still remaining in the world at large. As we no longer bow down before religious, genetic, political, military, scientific, legal, or economic forms of authority, which have revealed their insanity more and more with each passing day, we have had to go and look within ourselves in order to access soul revelations that are of a more credible nature. We no longer want to be told what to do with our lives by the minds of others. We now want to discover and understand what a fruitful and congruent life means for ourselves.

But without the monastic walls to protect us, it has become all the more important to find a suitable training ground for inner contemplation and prayer so that we do not become lost and overwhelmed by the ceaseless agitations of everyday life. On this training ground we come to get our bearings straight whenever we feel lost from ourselves and it is where we turn to whenever we feel the need to anchor ourselves again in the ways of our spirit and soul. Our training ground is our therapy couch and it is also the place we come to contemplate the mysteries of this life. It is the place where we may eventually realise what a fruitful life means for us. Our training ground, whatever it may be, becomes the foundation stone upon which our life in the world is steadily built.

For some the foundation stone is a time of silent prayer at the beginning and at the end of the day. For others it is a time of meditation each morning that helps them become centred and balanced for the day ahead. For others it is reading a sacred text or listening to a piece of music that speaks to their heart, leads them inwards, and renews their soul whenever they feel drained or overwhelmed. For me though the foundation stone was planted through playing golf.

I am grateful to have this opportunity to share my reflections and experiences of twenty years practice on the golf course. It is through these experiences that I discovered that the golf course is my safe place of refuge between the kingdoms of God and man, and to my surprise, I realised that it is on the golf course that I really began to learn and grow in the ways of my soul. It is the vehicle that first navigated me safely through on that journey into my interior landscape.

This surprising realisation came in hindsight only recently. As Murphy muses in his own writings, it is quite bizarre to try and imagine some of the great teachers throughout our history slinging a bag of golf clubs on their back and heading out onto the course. It just doesn't seem an obvious place to come and take that kind of sacred journey.

So before I had this realisation it is fair to say that outside of the golf course I had been consciously entertaining the mysteries of my soul for at least the past ten years after realising that there must be so much more to 'who I am' than the self I'd been told I was. It was a time where I was moving swiftly from authority to inquiry. But at the beginning of my conscious search, I did not know that a decade before I'd been already been preparing myself for this opening after having entered the mysterious world of golf. It was as if these ten years of experience on the golf course had been quietly preparing me for this more conscious period of inquiry, and though it sounds bold, it may not be an exaggeration to say that I've been taught more life lessons through my time on the golf course than through my time in the school classroom. I truly feel grateful then that I found this training ground and that it has allowed me to put down a solid foundation stone in the world.

If you have a passion for golf then you may find that these writings offer a new perspective on the game that you hadn't been aware of before. Others may be aware of the mystical teachings to be drawn from this sport; but perhaps this book can take you deeper into it. However, in truth, these writings are not really about the virtues of the game of golf and I have no interest in persuading you to take up the sport. We each have to find our own vehicle that best supports us through the ups and downs of daily life and that helps us find meaning in it. We each have to find our own special key that opens the door to grace.

The inspiration for these writings is to *encourage you the reader to find your key*. Yet, paradoxically, we really do not have to look hard for it usually comes to find us first whenever we are ready to receive *that* call from the Divine. All we have to do is be open to the signs and listen to where it is our soul moves us. In my case the sign was illuminated when, at the age of three, I moved home and found myself living only a five minute walk from the gates of the local golf club. Nine years later I started to become curious about what was to be found on the other side of that gate…and swiftly became a member. The game has 'hooked' me ever since (as you would probably guess from my strong left hand hooker's grip that naturally causes me to close the club head on impact rather than striking it square).

I hope to inspire you to become open to the signs by illuminating particular aspects of the journey that we all go on as we explore the nature of our souls through our practice. Although I will be describing it from behind the windscreen of my golfing vehicle, in truth, the process is the same whatever vehicle we use. Golf can, therefore, be treated simply as a *metaphor* that may easily be applied to all forms of inner inquiry into our souls. For once you go beyond the surface appearance and form of golf, and begin to speak with the *language of the soul*, you realise that the words used are applicable for all forms of contemplative practice.

In illuminating the journey through the game of golf I want to show you the rich language that this peculiar game can offer to the open mind. There is a choice to make here. We can choose to ignore the signs and focus on the superficiality and form of our training ground; much like we might choose to see a church as nothing more than a building made of brick. Or we can choose to take that journey and look a little deeper into the vast mysteries that always lie beneath and beyond the form.

The question is; are you ready to go with me even deeper down the rabbit hole?

R.A. Moseley
July 2012

The Arrival

I had seen him come to the gates many times before with that longing look in his eye. He always stopped and turned his head towards the driveway, which snaked its way through this lush green landscape that I call home. But I knew he could not see me waiting here for I knew that he was not yet ready to see me. Little did he know or understand what was drawing his attention and I knew that he would simply turn and walk away once more and go back to the place that was known to him. The hour was not yet at hand; but it was close and the sense of anticipation was hanging heavy in the air.

I longed to run to those gates and to call his name forth. I longed to speak with him and to say it was safe to cross over. Oh how much unnecessary time is lost in the chaos of the world that lies beyond those gates! If only he knew what I knew then he would not waste another second out there in the wilderness. He is fighting for scraps when all the while there is such a delicious banquet to be found in here! But I resist for I am ever patient. I know that it is scripted this way and that all must unfold in its own good time. One day he will surely heed the call of the golf course.

But although it is scripted; I know that the moment of recognition may not come of his own choosing. There are none out there to help point him this way anymore and it will be almost by random chance or strange coincidence that he will happen to stumble on through. And I know all too well that the distractions from the seducing whirl of a chaotic world are surely hard ones for him to resist on his own. Danced into delusion, how can I possibly expect him to stop and glimpse the power of the still and spacious void that lies within here? All the while then the whole world devilishly weaves its web of illusion around him; entrapping him in its forms and its attachments. It is truly cunning in its seduction and I know that out there he is nothing more than a powerless puppet that is being pulled up and down on a string by the twisted hand of fear. He is like so many in the world today who appear comfortable and content but who are not truly living the life they were born to live. They are the voyeurs standing on the river bank watching as their life passes them by.

Sadly then, not one authentic word has ever passed his lips and not one spontaneous movement has occurred in all that he has said and done in that world beyond these gates. If only he would break free of these strings he would surely see that there was another way. But alas, this is the way it is and this is the way it must go.

However, though the situation all sounds depressingly gloomy, I know that no matter how tightly the web is woven around; the call of the Divine, when it comes, will shatter it all in an instant. There is simply nothing on earth that can stop or resist the sacred hour when it strikes to cut through the veil of illusion. It may come in the form of tragedy: a heart attack, a doctor's diagnosis, the loss of a loved one; or it may come in the form of beauty and awe; a baby's birth, a stumble onto hallowed ground, or a sacred gift from nature's tender hand. But who can possibly predict beforehand how it will all come about! It is none of my business and all I can do is sit and wait for that clarion call to sound!

In the meantime he toys with me whilst I patiently stand by the white flag that flutters at the heart of the 17th green, the hole closest to the entry gate, and keep open the invitation of surrender to the game and its mysteries. Again and again he comes; and again and again he goes. I watch it all like watching the tide that ebbs and flows. How little does he know that I will wait here for the whole of eternity if I must.

But then in an unplanned moment the destined hour arrives

and storm clouds appear and hang low overhead. It all comes about so swiftly and I can see that he is now ready to burst forward across the threshold. He has heard the call; I am sure of it. Courage now fills his open heart and I hear the swish of a knife cutting through those puppet strings that had propped him up for so long. Oh how I've longed to hear that sweetest of sounds for how much sheer delight it brings me when the hour of catharsis arrives! Thunder rumbles overhead in its appreciation and flashes of lightning strike to reveal the electricity of the moment.

He is vulnerable and I can feel the earth tremble as he stumbles forward across it. He is alone and no-one on this earth has come to help him cross over and to honour this most sacred and intimate moment in his life. Feelings of guilt are like vines wrapped around his feet as he comes face-to-face with the resistance of a world that is trying to smother him and pull him backwards into their arms. I cannot step in and interfere here but I need not fear for the momentum of change is so strong that nothing can now stop it. Some part of him is going to die tonight; and whilst the world mourns the child it has lost...it is the hour of celebration for the Gods at the sight of the man that is ready to be reborn!

He finally wrenches himself through the tangled bonds of human resistance; and now stands naked on the other side of the gate. Finally I have him here all alone and it is time to get reacquainted. Finally I can show my face and he will now surely see me standing here before him.

But although there is a flicker of recognition as I come close; his gut instinct leads him to take a big step back. The habits of earthly survival continue to serve him well but he is wise enough to stay rooted on this side of the gate; for the moment at least. On some level he knows that once he'd crossed over that threshold that there can be no going back. Having finally dipped his toes in the river he knows he will have to immerse himself in its current right until the very end. It is all or nothing now.

He is nervous; not of me I think, but more of the virgin sound of silence that he has never tasted before. For so long he has been marching to the beat of someone else's drum that I know it will take time for him to recover now that the drum has finally stopped its rhythmic boom-boom beat.

'Who are you?' he asks with a tremor of trepidation in his voice as he looks upon the shadow of my looming presence that is cast over him.

'What Virgil was to Dante; I am to you. I am the one who can guide you safely through this labyrinth you have come to.'

'But please tell me your name?' he asks earnestly.

'You can name me the same as the one who inspires you the most; the one who has helped turn your head to the light of the heavens.'

'Oh,' he says with shoulders dropping in disappointment. 'There are none I know who I hold in such reverence as that.'

'Then I shall remain the nameless one. But worry not for names are not very important here. The real question is whether you recognise my face at all?'

'You do seem vaguely familiar it is true…but I can't at all place where I know you from,' he stutters back confusedly.

'You and me were once together in the stars,' I answer looking dreamily towards the sky above.

'The stars? Is that where I have returned then?' he asks bewilderedly with eyes that scanned slowly across a strange and unfamiliar horizon.

'Not yet no; but sometime soon you will. For now though your feet remain rooted to this earth and breath continues to come into your body. You have not died because you have not yet lived. I am simply here to remind you of what you have forgotten before you can even think of returning home.'

'Well please tell me then; what is this place?'

'You like to call this sanctuary a golf course; but for me it is a halfway house where we can safely meet each other. You see, I can't come out into your world and you are not yet ready to return to

12

mine. This golf course serves then as a bridge between our two worlds and perhaps for this reason you often find it placed out here on the neglected strip of land that exists between the kingdoms of town and country; and of man and nature.'

'But why have I been led here?'

'To play this game so that you may begin to recognise again who you truly are. There is so much you need to remember that you have forgotten and this halfway house is designed to be a perfect training ground to teach you all that you need to know.'

'So if I master this game you will take me back to the stars?' he asks wide-eyed and with his imagination suddenly captured by the possibility of release from the bonds that tie him down to the earth.

'Not quite yet,' I answer ruefully. 'I am here to teach you how to live a more congruent life in the world you've come from; and it is only when you have fulfilled your mission on earth that you can return home. I want you to see the golf course more as a place that has been designed to speed the process along by getting your life back on track...more than treating it as just another exit gate.'

'It does feel so strange here though. I'm not sure if I really want to go any further,' he says hesitantly with one fearful eye still turned back towards the gate he has come through.

'That's only because the rules here feel very different to the rules out there.'

'And why is that so?' he answers impatiently.

'In here we are ruled by the three mysterious and elusive qualities of silence, spaciousness, and the eternal timeless now. These qualities are strange to you because they are not at all known in the world you have just come from. Out there speed and efficiency are of the utmost importance in your life. Look and you will see how much you fill your days with multitudes of tasks. Always doing, doing, doing; and always cast under the spell of the wandering mind. That is the world you know. But here in the sanctuary of the golf course that world is swiftly turned upside down. This is a game that spans across many acres and across many hours; and if you come with me you will see that in this span of space and time *that not a lot happens.* Speed and efficiency are meaningless qualities out here and if the task of golf is to hit a little white ball into a hole; then during the game you will only be performing that task at a fraction of the time spent on the course. Indeed; putting the forms of the golf course in comparison to the spaciousness of the golf course is like putting the forms of the stars in comparison to the spaciousness of the cosmos.'

'But why do I need to come and play by these rules?'

'Because as I've told you already; I can't work with you out on the other side of the gate when you are too busy playing by the rules of noise and haste! The only place there is going to be room for me in your life in this world is right here in this halfway house.'

'But you haven't yet given me a good reason why I need you in my life!'

'I am needed because I can help you stand alone on your own two feet and to break free of all that holds you down in fear. Only here in the spacious, silent and eternal now can I teach you to look within and to know your true face. Only here can I help unmask the real authentic you.'

'Look hold on a minute here!' he reacts with strained panic against my bold invitation. 'I'm just a regular guy here going about my business and trying to make a decent and honest life for myself. I don't quite know how I ended up here but this whole self-absorbed navel-gazing business is surely not for me!'

'You can't live a meaningful life out there in any other way,' I insist firmly.

'But I am living a good life out there!' he reacts even more strongly. 'I work hard at an honest worthwhile job, I have a beautiful wife and family, and I own a breathtaking home and a luxurious car. Can you not see that from here? I also look out for my friends, I care for my elderly folks, I pay my taxes, I donate to charities when I can; so what more of a life do you want me to make!' he adds

14

whilst compiling his golden list upon his fingers.

'These will all turn to ash one day,' I respond soberly. 'There's nothing solid in that list from which to build a life upon. Deep down you know this because that's why you have come here. You are ready for the truth that is permanent.'

He falls silent as if not knowing how to respond to my cutting remark. He clearly doesn't yet know this to be true and he is deflated, and not liberated, in even thinking of his golden life turning to ash. I must carry on with a little more tact.

'Look; as long as your days are determined and directed by the outer circumstances of your life then you will remain conditioned by the objects that constantly capture your attention. You may be tempted to think that a busy, productive and dutiful life in the world is highly rewarding. You may think that you are being of valued service to the world by being out there performing all the time and making a good fist of things. Maybe those strings that pull you to do the things you think you should be doing; *do* help you to be of merit. Who can say? All I know is that it is not what you do, but the quality of the consciousness that goes into what you do, that really matters in the end. Believe me when I say that it is only to the extent that you have cut the strings and grasped this game that you can then return and be truly of service in the world. For if you don't then you can only really be a robot servant who performs effective lip service in their roles but whose heart is never engaged in what they do. There surely can be no genuine authenticity, creativity or power in your actions. There can be no lasting success.'

'So you think I have come here because I know all of this?' he asks doubtfully.

'Not consciously perhaps; but there is some part of you that is ready to hear this truth. There is some part of you that resonates with what I say for I can promise you that you would not be here if you were not searching for something more substantial than this life of dutiful lip service that you call living.'

'But the last thing I wanted was to hear *him* call my name,' he surprisingly admits in a rare moment of unabashed honesty that cuts right through to the heart of his resistance.

'Well that's true for everyone who crosses through the gate and leaves behind a life that is known for one that has no planned future or guaranteed outcome. You are scared because you know that when he spoke to you that you would have to make the greatest sacrifice of your life.'

'But I don't want to give up everything just to become a cloistered moth eaten monk!' he reacts with pained anguish.

I cannot help but laugh in astonishment. I am utterly fascinated to see what stories the mind spins in order to keep us safely away from the golf course. A cloistered moth eaten monk indeed!

'You really don't have to. I am not here to take you away from the world into a place of distant retreat behind a monastery wall. Quite the opposite in fact. I am here to teach you how to live more fully in the world; to teach you how *to be in this world but not of this world.* Yes I admit that by the end of our game there may be things from your old life that you will need to let go of because you will have outgrown them; but I promise that you will renounce them willingly by choice and not because I expect it of you. You will renounce them because you will know that whatever comes to fill its vacant place will be so much richer and more fulfilling than you can possibly imagine. Surely you must wish to fulfil your true earthly potential and to not waste another minute living a life you were not born to live?'

'It does sound lovely,' he concedes as he finally allows the feelings of his heart to pass comment. 'But I know I have just left a lot of unhappy people behind me in coming even this far,' he whimpers powerlessly to shut it closed.

'Don't take that as a sign that you are off the right path. Know that all those who have ever come to play this game have been made outcast by those on the other side of the gate who can no longer handle your challenging presence in the flock.'

'But I have no desire to be difficult and problematic to those I love and care deeply about! How can you think that I am such a threat to them?'

'Because you are merely a projection of their own fears and your courage to follow that call through the gate challenges them just as deeply as it has challenged you. In fact it challenges them more because they are not yet ready to act upon their disillusionment.'

'A projection? You make it sound as if I don't even exist in their eyes!' he reacts; as if stung by the idea that he truly is of no importance to those who once seemed close to him. 'I always thought that my family and friends wanted the best for me,' he finished limply.

'They want the best; but only as long as you stay in the confines of the box they have placed both themselves and you within. Isn't that what tribal relationships are all about? Are they not built solely on mutual interests you share together? And if so, is it not natural for those relationships to dissolve when one person decides to leave that box behind and to move on to other things?'

'No I simply can't agree with that! True friends would surely be able to adapt and grow through the changes.'

'But only if both people are willing to change together. If only one is willing then the other would be forced to confront his own unwillingness if he were to stay in close contact. Every time both people met from then on would simply be an agony for him and that is why he unhappily drifts away and does not come to watch you cross over. For the person who was once a friend has now become a threat because his willingness to change calls into question the established order of life within the confines of the box and which have long been accepted as the norm. But though it seems painful for the one left behind; don't use that as an excuse to not change yourself for no-one will escape the hand of suffering if you neglect to follow your heart's natural impulse out of fear of upsetting others.'

'But there must be an easier and less painful way of going about this,' he pleads. 'I don't want them to think of me as a threat.'

'It isn't your place to interfere,' I warn. 'Your business is to follow your own heart; and you must trust that in the end your example will help others to cross that gate too. Don't judge or try to change their beliefs. For now you must let them go and let them be.'

'But if coming here is such a glorious occasion in the life journey of a human being; then why is it not marked and celebrated as such *right now*? Why does it have to feel like an act of betrayal?'

'I am marking and celebrating it along with all the heavenly hosts that I represent. The whole of this cosmos is united and is screaming 'yes' in a raised crescendo at this meeting that is taking place right now. Is that not enough for you? Does one person's fearful *opinion* really matter more than all of that?'

He immediately falls silent as he struggles to comprehend and appreciate the magnitude of blessing that he is receiving right now. He is struggling to shift his perspective and to wriggle free of this cloak of guilt that he has wrapped around himself.

'How can I possibly trust that what you are saying is true?' he finally asks the inevitable question to the one he has become estranged from for too long.

'Because the day has come when the risk of remaining tight in the bud is more painful than the risk it takes to blossom,' I respond gravely whilst holding out my hand towards him. 'Sometimes you just have to take a leap of faith. Coming here was one. Continuing is another,' I add mysteriously.

'So I can't just have a look around on my own,' he asks peeking curiously up the driveway; still unsure how far he is willing to leap.

'No. It is only I who knows the territory of the golf course and who can lead you around. Now take my hand and I can show you what a soulful life gives as opposed to the soulless one you know. You may not trust me fully yet but I assure you that you will in time.'

'But you do at least promise that it is safe for me out there?' he asks still wavering in uncertainty about whether he is ready to commit or not.

'Absolutely not! Don't let me delude you for one second into thinking that this is going to be at all pleasant or comfortable for you. Transformation never is and never will be that. This is going to be the toughest ride of your life because in the midst of the fire you are about to enter; all that you cherish now in that mind of yours will most likely get burned away to nothing.'

'Well that just sounds absolutely horrible! Why do you expect me to want to go through all of that?'

'Because when the fire has done its work what will be left in the embers is the shining jewel of your being; the never changing truth of who you really are. It is the treasure that lies waiting for you deep within; and if that is all you now want then you really have to be willing to go through the fire to get it.'

With that the penny has finally dropped. He wants the treasure; that much he is now ready to admit. The question is whether he is willing to give absolutely everything to get it? Is he willing to take that kind of ultimate risk?

'Come let us go to the first hole and we can begin our journey together from there,' I say offering out the hand of invitation again.

He finally nods his head in agreement and takes hold. Though the road ahead is long, and though the roots of his commitment are not yet sown deep, I am simply enchanted by this time of reconnection. In his innocent presence here I cannot help but twirl and swoon my way up the driveway; and all the while leading him along on my merry dance.

An Opening

We walk by the old rundown timber framed pro shop that sits adjacent to the more austere double storey red brick clubhouse. Inside the window there are many wonderful little gadgets that proudly showcase man's ingenuity of mind and which are guarded by the club professional who presides here as there most faithful servant. But I have little to do with him and his fancy tools and so I choose to keep my bag of clubs outside the shop window and away from his watchful eye. He has little time or appreciation for my way of teaching…and I have little time or appreciation for his. However, later on in our game he will be needed to play his part and so I have to show some respect that he has his purpose for being here. I know all too well that there is no-one or no-thing to be found out on this golf course by random chance.

Hearing the sound of footsteps he comes keenly to the door and we give each other a mutual nod of recognition. Knowing it is me he doesn't linger though to speak. Instead, as he walks away, I turn back to my new companion and give a warm smile as I take hold of my bag of clubs that have been sat waiting for this most auspicious of occasions. I am silent for a moment as I cast my eyes down upon them with reverence. The jovial atmosphere has subsided with the solemn change in mood I am deliberately creating here.

'You are free to borrow these but they must be returned here when we are done,' I say with clear intent.

He walks closer to inspect my bag which reveals to him an

odd and misshapen collection of clubs that I have worked with from the very beginning. His face soon drops in unmasked disappointment for he'd clearly hoped to be given the most impressive set of clubs to come out here and play with. He looks longingly towards the shop window where a big booming driver hangs down on show and then looks back at my old chipped piece of metal whose club head was only the size of a fist. He falls quiet for a moment as if wondering whether it would be impolite to refuse and to ask for something better.

'Jeez, how on earth did you learn to play with these? Are they coated with special fairy dust or something?' he finally asks jokingly as if to try and lighten the mood without offending at the same time. I am still a stranger and he is evidently unsure how to be around me.

'These clubs will get you around the course but let me say that they possess no magic powers to help you play the game any better here than on any other. Man is always trying to use his cunning mind to design the perfect set of clubs and the perfect golf ball so as to bypass all the challenges that the golf course offers. I offer no such promise. You must go and face the course naked.'

He falls silent again as if unsure how to react to being so brusquely scolded for his impudence. He longs to debate the matter further but I can see he is holding his tongue.

'Yes master,' was all that he muttered quietly as he probably decided that it was best to proceed cautiously with me at the moment.

'Come let us walk then. The first hole is awaiting us.'

He takes the bag from my hand and follows a step behind as we walk on towards the first tee. But once we arrive at the end of the path, I feel to take a step to the side and to let him pass by. For having taken that most difficult first step across the threshold, I'm well aware that my companion is now walking with a lot more assurance in his stride. He may be uncertain about my guiding presence; but out here he can at least no longer hear the siren songs

21

of the outside world. I can tell that he is already beginning to bask in the virgin newness of this experience. It isn't so jarring and strange anymore and for the first time in his life he is beginning to get a taste for the silent, spacious and eternal now. Despite his initial fears about coming here, there is something in the energetic resonance of the golf course that is lifting his spirits effortlessly into a harmonious and peaceful state. He is recognising that everything feels so naturally at ease and in its rightful place here as I know that for now this halfway house has been well designed to provide him with a welcome place to call home.

Here on the first tee he can see how the hole has been especially designed to welcome. There is a wide fairway sloping steeply downhill from the teeing area into a bowl shape to gather the golf ball into the centre at the bottom. The attractive slope tempts the golfer to come and play his shot as even the ball struck askew may find itself coming to rest in the perfect spot to approach the green. From the bottom of the slope it is only a short approach to the flat putting surface. The flag positioned in the centre of the large green looks easily approachable and inviting. This is clearly a hole where the novice is encouraged to come and have a go.

I watch as he pulls the driver out from the golf bag and swings it freely a few times. Feeling comfortable, he then approaches the ball that looks up invitingly from its perch on a wooden peg. The white dimply surface glows under the reflection of the sun and seems to captivate his attention fixatedly. Although he is not used to playing with such a meagre looking club; it seems easy in this moment for him to obey the first rule of golf by keeping his eye firmly on the ball as he brings the club back and through to send it flying sweetly towards the target.

He bends down to pull the tee peg from the earth; and then saunters down the sloping path ahead as if suddenly oblivious to my guiding presence here. I worry not though for I know that my time to step in will soon come. In the meantime I can let him walk on and enjoy the immediate response from his commitment to come and play the game here with me. I can see that his beginner's mind is open and ready to receive the fruits of the game instantaneously.

We eventually come to where the ball lies invitingly at the bottom of the slope on a flat smooth surface. Not even a pro like me would have chosen a better spot for my ball to rest. From here there is barely a hundred yards distance left between the ball and the hole and so it only requires a gentle wedge to reach the target. He approaches confidently, but as I knew it would, somewhere in this moment his game goes awry and the sweet bliss of the ripened fruit begins to turn horribly sour. He swung back and around freely enough; but as he brought the shaft down and through, the club head merely clanged on impact and sent the ball squirting off low and to the right. It was a glorious and not-so-pretty shank as handed down by the golfing Gods.

He looks up at me aghast and in embarrassment at his surprising error.

'There's nothing to worry about with that,' I speak reassuringly. 'It's just showing you that you need to play with your heart as well as your head.'

'I don't understand. I played it no differently than my drive,' he answered; still puzzled by what had just happened.

'If you'd been hammering in some nails to a board and then needed to get a screwdriver to put in some screws; you wouldn't continue to use the hammer would you?'

'What do you mean?'

'The long game of golf is completely different from the short game of golf; that's what I mean.'

'So I need to swing differently; is that what you are saying?'

'It's not just your swing; it's your whole approach. Look, let me tell you up front that where you've come from you've been taught to relate to life very much through your mind,' I answer pointing my finger against my temple. 'You are taught to relate to life through the filters of mental abstraction rather than relate to it directly. So even though it may well look to you as if you have crossed the threshold from that world; sadly you are still carrying

23

the tools from that place with you and you are still trying to play the game with them here.

'But let me tell you that if you keep trying to play *this* game with your mind in sole charge; then nothing new can possibly be learned or created out here. You will simply recreate old patterns of behaviour and the cost of your over-intellectualisation will keep on coming to you in the form of the shanks. It happens because you are approaching the ball and the golf swing too rigidly and too mechanically. You are approaching your game far too abstractly.'

'So what must I do differently?'

'The only way then to really succeed out here is to learn how to *feel*; you need to learn how to approach your game experientially, to actually feel the shot, and not just play it intellectually. Now you can perhaps get away with using the old set of mind tools when playing the long game – at least for a while - but it can only serve you for part of your game. Ultimately it won't be of any help to you in sinking the ball into the hole.'

A moment's silence falls between us as he tries to grasp what it means to feel his way through the game. 'There is a powerful slogan my master taught me when I first learned to play the game which helped me a lot with understanding this,' I add.

'What slogan was that?' he asks keenly.

'*You drive for show but you putt for dough*,' I reply simply.

'I don't get it?' he asks blankly.

'What it means is that your heart is the source of your power and strength; not your mind or its will. Although you've been encouraged to think that success comes from your head; it is really all show and no substance. True lasting success only comes when you curb your mind and learn to listen to this mysterious power and to follow its leadings. If you want to get your ball into the hole you need to develop a new skill in your armoury. You need to learn how to feel intuitively.'

He listens and looks at me as if I have just asked him something absurd; as if he is a fish who is suddenly being asked to fly.

'You want me to play this game without my mind? Are you crazy!'

I ignore this comment and throw another ball down to the ground to get him to try the shot again. Another glorious shank followed and I could see in his frustration that he needed more instruction with the technique.

'Don't take your struggles personally for your kind have all been brought up in this Dark Age of Shank. Just take a look throughout the recent history of human civilisation and you will see how intuitives have been consistently persecuted by a mind-controlled world that has long associated them with the work of the devil. Is it any wonder you don't have the skills at hand to play the short game of golf when there has been no-one left in your world to teach you how to play direct from the heart? Come let me show you what I mean.'

I throw another ball on the ground and take the club from his hand.

'First of all you've got to start speaking a different language if you want to master this shot. You've got to start speaking the words of a lover for in the short game of golf we have to learn how to blend into a state of *oneness* with the club, the ball, the green, and the hole. Whereas your drive was to do with technique and timing; your wedge here is all to do with coaxing and touch. Soft and deli-cate hands are needed for the task,' I instruct as I try to demonstrate to him this ancient art of attunement. 'Try to imagine that you are the conductor who is trying to blend together all the different frag-ments into one unified and harmonised melody,' I add.

'It sounds beautiful,' he concurs as he watches. 'I just wish I had that level of skill to do it.'

'The more you practice the more sensitive you will become. It is like going onto a strange course and trying to take that first putt on the green. You have no clue as to the lie of the land and if that putt drops, or falls close to the hole, it will be by luck more than judgment. But the more you practice on that green the more sensi-

25

tively attuned you will become and your judgment will become ever more refined. But you have to be willing to listen and to adjust based on the feedback you receive.'

'To listen?' he asks curiously.

'Yes that's right; you have to listen in order to attune. Take a look at the golfer who is busy trying to master his chipping and putting through abstract mathematical formulas that reveal to him the precise line and length to take. Such a golfer will never succeed because he is too busy ruminating in his head to listen to what the green is revealing to him in his heart. Like I say you have to get a feel not a thought for it. And let me add that the short game of golf can be a deeply sensual experience for the one who can truly feel it.'

With that I give the club a smooth gentle swing and send the ball gracefully towards its target.

'Do you understand what I mean now?'

'Yes I see,' he answers; all the while looking across at me with wide and earnest eyes as if pleading to be given back the club and another ball. I can tell his heart has been starved of love and that his vocabulary of feelings does not go beyond the fingers on my hands. In the polite and ordered world he has come from; what I teach is seen as both enticing and dangerous because I blur the straight line edges and I tear down the protective walls that are placed around our hearts by rules and reason. I am the flirt who dares to dance with uncertainty and who risks getting consumed by my desire and heartbroken by my despair.

But I must resist the temptation to fuel his appetite. There are many starved individuals who spend years here in search of that bridge between the head and the heart. Some will even spend their whole lives here and never find the way through. One shanked wedge after another happens until in frustration they eventually give up the game completely. Little do they know that it is their own overzealous efforts that are barring them from the gate and giving them nothing more than a stiff neck in the process! Little do they know that the way of the heart is our natural and instinctive birthright and is not something that can be engineered and earned through hard endeavour and disciplined practice! In striking the shot over and over again they are foolishly trying to sharpen the hammer into a screwdriver...when the screwdriver is patiently sitting there next to them all the time. Such is the madness of the human mind!

'You can't stay stationary on the golf course; you always have to keep things moving through,' I say mysteriously as I break the spell and push us forwards to where his second shot had come to rest. I did this because I had the impression that the short walk may somehow help him to forget his controlling mind and would perhaps help him to stumble upon this birthright of his. Such is the beauty of golf that out here you don't have to dwell fixatedly on the object of your practice when there is so much spaciousness that lies around it; and I am the one here who knows that it is only in the spacious, silent and eternal now that the bridge will be found. Yes that's right. That bridge to the heart simply cannot be found through the forms of the game no matter how hard he may strive to reach that special state of attunement. But oh how baffling it would be to him at the moment if I told him that he will only find what he is truly searching for when his mind stops looking for it!

So I stay quiet and simply look across in wonderment as to whether he is truly ready to unearth that first taste of the attuned heart which would serve as a solid anchor for the rest of his game here. Or then again; will he merely shank the shot and be forced to stay on this first hole a little longer!

As he approaches the ball though I notice something beginning to shift in his energy field; much like a radio losing its static and being tuned into a crystal clear reception. I see this exact moment happen within his eyes as they open wide like a flower before the light of the sun. He is beginning to feel the nameless force; and with this he is slowly glimpsing the deliciously simple, and yet subtle, teaching of this first hole.

Tuned in then with this clarity of spacious awareness, which has definitely added a new dimension to his level of perception, he

27

comes to hover over the ball at his feet. Once there he begins to merge and to become one with the force itself. Boundaries are falling away and he surely no longer knows where he begins and ends. It is all becoming one. Softly, softly then he lets his knees bend and the shoulders sink as he relaxes fully into this moment. I watch all of this take place with a few silent words of encouragement under my breath.

He cannot name what is happening here but I can see that everything is falling into perfect alignment with his heartfelt intent for the shot ahead. He has fallen away deep into the spacious void and in this void he is graced to receive his first genuine spiritual opening that tears its way through his entire being. The club moves, the ball is struck, it lands, rolls gently across the green, and nestles down right by the side of the hole. He can't at all say how it has happened; but the result is that he is now left with only the shortest of tap-ins for a glorious opening par four!

'What on earth have I been missing,' he says quietly to himself as he savours the taste of this precious moment that has sent tingles of aliveness pulsing through his body. These are the words that will cement his place here on the golf course and a sacred longing has been stirred that can never now be ignored. He can no longer return and carry on lying to himself that all you see, hear, taste, touch and smell in this world is all that you get. He has now touched upon a mystical realm that has taken him far beyond the mundane view of things that he once knew.

I must contain my enthusiasm though. Rare is the person who finishes their game on the very first hole. He has had his taster but we have a lot more work to do before he can be immersed fully into the sacred flow of the golf course. The mind is truly cunning in its control over his life and I have to respect that it will not give up its hold on his heart so easily. However, despite this sombre warning of what is to come, I cannot help but let a big satisfying grin fall upon my face. Yes divinity may have descended down to earth to pull him through the threshold; but now he is the one ascending to meet his divinity right here on the golf course and in all of its heavenly glory. This is a sweet moment of intimacy that brings tears to my eyes. I am the matchmaker who has brought two lovers together and who has just seen them embrace for the very first time.

Peeking into the Inferno

He is standing firmly rooted and transfixed on the spot of his third shot and I know that he is going to need a lot of coaxing in order to sink that putt and to move on with his game. I know that he cannot cling on to this grand mystical state of consciousness for there is still much work for him to do. Harsh as it may seem; if he chooses to stay here he will only regress into his memories.

'What did I just tell you about not staying stationary on the course?' I ask sharply to lift him right out of his sweet reverie.

'But it is so nice here; can't I just stay a little longer?' he answers back in a soft dreamy tone.

'Let it go,' was my response in an even firmer voice.

He seemed utterly shocked by my jarring words for he thinks that he has just found the treasure that I had brought him here to see. And yet here I am now telling him to leave it alone!

'But why can't I stay here?' he now pleads more demandingly with me as he begins to doubt again whether he can really trust me as his guide. He is on the verge of setting up camp here and of refusing to go any further; even though our reunion has barely begun.

'Yes you know now what it is that is so attractive about this game. You know what drives the eccentric golfer to come out onto the course on a wet and freezing cold winter morning to hit a tiny white ball across a big field into little small holes. He comes in *faith* because he is hungry for that one special shot that will satisfy this deep longing you have come upon. This golfer is the one who comes out time and time again to hit that third shot on the first green in the hope that they will be able to hit that shot like they did sometime ago in the distant past. They are the ones hoping to re-enact and to keep alive a memory of mystical union that has been stored away deep inside.'

'Exactly! And what's so wrong with that!' he interjects. 'My God I've been living in such a wasteland if that feeling is anything to judge it by. Why should I not desire more of what I've just tasted?'

'Because I'm telling you that this isn't what the game is ultimately all about. Take a deeper look and you will see that beneath that sparkle in their eye; that these are lost souls who have become consumed by the addictive lure of the spiritual high and who have been overpowered by the return of the sensual lover in their lives. They are the ones who will look for anything that takes them back to this state of consciousness they've tasted on the first hole – be it hallucinogenic substances, sex, yoga, transcendental meditation, or even a golden trip to India. Though they seek the fulfilment of their longing they will never be satisfied when it is given and they will constantly seek for more.

It is perfectly apt that they find themselves stuck on the fringes of the first green for they are the ones today who just hang around on the fringes of society dreaming of peace and the summer of love they once savoured. They are the ones who will refuse to sink that par putt and to carry on with the game because they fear that if the ball disappears down into the depths of the hole that the experience may never touch them again. They are the ones who have inertia to growing up and moving on with their game and their life. The question is then; do you really want to be like them and to stay here like a demanding little child in a sweetshop?'

My words do not satisfy for the cloud of addiction hangs heavy between us. I know that he is not really willing to listen to my words of warning and his feet remain sunk deep into the soft and freshly mowed grass. Playing the scolding parent never seems to work well with children like these. I know that I am going to have to get into his shoes and to tempt him away with a more attractive offer.

'Look; I know that your resistance to move on with the game comes because it is not easy to come back into the limitations of this earthly body when you have just experienced the sheer vastness of the universe; when you have just experienced the *one*. You don't want to send that ball down into the depths of this constricted hole because the cold reality of your flesh and bone surely feels far too limiting for the spirit that has been unleashed and set free here on the first hole. I completely understand why you don't want the responsibility and the heaviness that is there if you do come back down into the confines of the earth.'

'That's exactly right! I do feel as if I have just climbed a humongous mountain and I am standing here at the top tasting the clean air and savouring the crystal clear sky! It is heavenly compared to the soupy and polluted atmosphere of the world below - and your right; I never want to descend again!'

'But descend you must because you must take that heavenly taste right back down to flush out the very depths of your psyche. Heaven should never be confined to one exalted place; it needs to pervade every moment and every corner of your life.'

'But if I could only stay here then it will have pervaded every moment and every corner without any further effort on my part!'

'Gravity will ensure that you will fall if you should try to dig your heels in. It is the law of the land. Much better to make the descent by choice now than wait for the inevitable push, don't you agree?'

'But how can you be so certain that I can't stay here?'

'Because this is an eighteen hole golf course…and you have not yet completed the first. I know what lies ahead and I know of the many riches that are yours to claim should you ever get to the end of the game. Don't be satisfied with these few trinkets given to you at the beginning of your quest and that will only rust away in time.'

Finally he perks up and is coaxed forward by my tempting words of treasures greater than this. How little does he know that I am playing on his addiction and will soon reveal to him that things are not going to turn out quite like he imagines they will! But for now I have piqued his curiosity and he is finally willing to go ahead and to sink that par putt. Now that it is done, and the score has been marked, it is time for me to get brutally honest. I wait though until we have reached the teeing area of the second before I speak again.

'Welcome to the second hole. This marks the beginning of your incarnating spirituality and the moment where we begin to do the ashes work of shining the light on your shadow side. This hole is about facing and working through your own hypocrisy that exists because of the schism that has been created between spirit and matter. It is here that I must remind you that you were given this contract of incarnation here into Earth school. You agreed to come down in order to take on your share of the collective unconscious with the task of transforming it with the light of your consciousness. You agreed to bring spirit into matter rather than separate spirit from matter. You agreed to reveal the light of the Divine through this world of form and to help advance the evolution of conscious-ness on this planet by becoming a channel for grace here. Your sacred promise when coming down the mountain at the time of your birth was to postpone your enlightenment until every other living soul has awakened. It is time to reaffirm this commitment by carrying on with your game…and to renounce your desire to bale back into the cosmos at this very first opportunity.'

My words are tough for him to digest but they are necessary ones for him to hear if he is to continue any further with this game. In truth there can be no pussyfooting around or dipping of toes out here on the difficult holes to come.

'I don't remember making any such promise!' is his first de-fensive response for he is instinctively wary of this weighty commit-ment that he is being asked to renew. I can tell that he is beginning to smell something fishy with the whole deal he has committed to but which he cannot easily turn back from now. All he has before him is my promise of greater treasures on this road ahead and he is weighing up again in his mind whether the reward still outweighs the risk. Oh how far he has to go before he is ready to stand here alone and free from his agendas! After his exalting mystical experience that happened barely a flicker ago he is back to asking his stock question of *'what's in it for me?'* Having tasted the complete freedom of the universe he is back down to his known self-interested world of limitation and separation.

'Well please tell me what you thought your purpose was for this existence of yours?' I respond warmly and with a wry humorous smile.

'I don't know,' he stumbles back in reply. 'I've never really given it much thought. I guess I've just never heard that line of argument from my peers before...' he admits openly.

'Yes but your peers can't even see the mountain you are coming down from; so what more do you expect from them? Now I'll be honest with you that it's kind of the deal around here. If you've tasted the sweet glory of the first then you have to take the responsibility of the second...and also the other holes to come.'

'Well you could have told me all this before heading out on the course!' he cusses as if still tasting the lingering feelings of betrayal from my persuading words that had led him away from the highs of the first. These are words that already seem hollow to him now.

'You knew and accepted all this way back in the beginning; and let me tell you that you did come down to this earth with your eyes wide open. Just remember that I am here simply to remind you all that you have forgotten when your eyes fell shut.'

'Did I really?' he asks doubtfully. 'But it all sounds like a lot of heavy and hard work though; this messy business of tackling all the suffering of the world and of helping advance the evolution of consciousness on this planet. I thought coming here was all about my self realisation and the treasure I would get out of it,' he continues on sullenly in the same selfish manner.

'Arrogance like that will get you nowhere around here. This is a place only for the humble at heart so speak no more like that with me or we will go no further together. No further at all. All you need to know is that a part has been assigned for you to play and you must quietly do your best to fulfil it. This is quite simply a 'no questions asked' directive from your maker.'

'But I surely have the choice whether to be here or not!' he protests; riding roughshod over my stark warning to curb his arrogance.

'No you don't,' I answer; mocking his bold words into submission. 'You are here by an act of Divine will and you cannot leave until that same Divine force dictates that the game is complete. Now yes I admit that you can choose to keep your eyes shut in ignorance and to drag it all out for the whole of eternity... or you can choose to open them and carry on with the game right now. That is the extent of your freedom. The question is; what will it be?'

He falls silent as if struck by the realisation that being here is going to be a lot, lot tougher than he first thought. He was also starting to realise that the guide who had seemed so warm and inviting at the beginning was becoming more and more impossibly demanding in his manner. But he also knew that he had no choice but to go on.

'How can the second hole teach me this incarnating spirituality?' he asks quietly as he slowly begins to yield to my forceful words.

'What will it be? I need to hear your spoken commitment first,' I reply; pulling him right back into the spotlight.

'Yes I will play my part,' he answers with prickly discomfort; and probably wondering how many more times he will have to prove his faith to me. Was crossing the gate not enough?

'Very good,' I answer approvingly. 'Now the second hole is only the beginning of a long road but here the starting point of your commitment is towards your own physical body. One of the consequences of the intoxication from the first hole is that your body suffered terribly when your spirit was trying to break free and be elsewhere. The neglect of one's own body on this journey is one of the greatest errors of our long spiritual past for it had been assumed that the poverty of asceticism was a necessity if we were to make progress on our soul's journey. But it is not the body and the material forms of this world that act as a hindrance in your quest for self realisation; *it is only your attachment to them.*

We will deal with these attachments later but first on this second hole you must realise that it is not healthy or wise to create this schism where your spirit is up in the heavens in a blissful meditative fairyland whilst your neglected body and mind continues to create hell on earth through mindless unconsciousness. You must find a way to honour and unite all of these within your practice if you are to make further progress on this course.'

He nods his head in acknowledgment and stands on the second tee with club in hand and ball teed up. Then, after a gentle practice swing, he stops, as if wondering how to go forth with my instruction.

'Well how can I begin to unite again my body, mind and spirit?' he turns his head towards me and asks.

'You must first begin on this hole by recognising the universal energetic force that your heart tapped into on the first and you must then work to harness and ground it as it moves through your earthly body. In traditional Chinese culture this force was called Qi and the Chinese have well established systems of philosophy and practice to work with this Qi in the body to bring about healing and wholeness. The primary intention here is to use this force to bring the body, mind, emotions, and spirit into a place of balance and order so as to restore us to a state of health and wellbeing.'

'Okay I can understand the basic idea of what you are saying. But how does that relate to golf?' he interrupts impatiently.

'Simply bring attention to your swing,' was my final pith instruction.

The second was a much more challenging hole than the first. It was both flatter and longer in length; even though it had the same recommended score for par as the first. It also contained a narrower fairway to navigate through with a few mature trees dotted alongside as it dog-legged slightly around to the left. The teeing area was raised a few feet and I walked around to watch closely the way of his swing with the ball resting between us.

I nodded my head appreciatively as I observed the many practice swings he was taking. He was starting to get a feel of the energy moving through his body and I can sense it becoming more grounded and rooted; it was becoming more balanced and contained. In observing I could clearly see the way the full golf swing offers a powerful movement that gets the Qi working through the body much in the same way that it does in the ancient oriental movement practices of Chi Kung and Tai Chi.

Feet standing square and balanced; knees slightly bent; a turn of the waist ninety degrees in one direction and then one-hundred and eighty degrees in the other; shoulders turning too; neck and head bent forward but held steady; arms raised then lowered and raised again in a flourish; elbows bending and extending; wrists given a gentle flick; ankles turning. Orchestrated together rhythmically into one great symphony; yes the full golf swing truly is a most majestic movement practice!

Finally he is ready to approach the shot, and by the transfer of energy from spirit to matter, the ball is sent away firmly enough in the right direction; where it just about holds on to the far edge of the left-hand fairway. But whereas he only had a wedge left to play on the first, he will need to play a longer iron in order to reach the green on this more challenging of holes. He returned the driver to the bag and we began to walk together in silence towards where the ball had come to rest. I looked over and could tell that he was still unsure as to the exact benefits of the instruction. His mind was in desperate need of some visible proof.

'Have you ever wondered why this game appeals to the elderly?' I ask.

'No, I can't say I have,' he responds as if puzzled by the question.

'It is because it is a rare sport that actually promotes good health in age rather than a sport that deteriorates it. You see one of the main challenges you will face as you get older is the loss of life energy circulating in your body as you begin to lose your vitality and your roots naturally wither as you prepare to leave this earth. Golf, however, is a gentle game that has long helped to keep the flow of Qi moving naturally through the body and has helped to keep joints well oiled and active into old age.

Of course though, as with everything, we have to be mindful of balance in our practice and it is also true that the one who spends hours hitting balls on the range may overdo things and create stress and tension in the body. Professional golfers can suffer from joint problems, which arise from too much forceful and repetitive strain.'

'Okay so coming out on the golf course can be good for my health if I don't overdo it. I can understand the idea of that. But I still don't understand what this all teaches me about this grand commitment of mine to come down the mountain and help save the world?'

'Stop trying to see the final picture when the jigsaw puzzle remains untouched in the box. Simply put each piece I give you into the puzzle and trust that it all has its place in the whole,' I reply mysteriously; and with a vain attempt at getting his mind to stop controlling everything so intensely.

We come to where his ball was at rest and I saw that he would need to adjust his swing in order to bend the ball around the trees that were blocking his direct line of approach. On this dog-legged hole his drive had gone too tightly to the left. However, there was a silver lining, as being in this spot would at least help him to keep his attention more tightly focused on his body and swing. We both knew that it is only in the correct movement of the golf swing that he would be able to achieve the desired shape and trajectory on the shot ahead.

He takes a six iron from his bag and I watch closely as he stands there toying with the shape of his swing. As he does so I can see that it is indeed helping to create a calming and stabilising influence upon him. Once comfortable, he takes a step forward and plays the shot. He is ultimately unsuccessful in drawing the ball back around far enough to the flag and it lands down in a hollow at the front right edge of the green; some twenty yards shy of the target. Although the shot did not achieve its desired outcome I can at least see that he is now ready for the next piece in the puzzle. Before he has chance to place the club into the bag; I take it from him and start to take a few swings myself.

'Not only do we find that the swing has a powerful grounding and stabling influence, as we stand here balanced with our feet firmly placed into the earth, but we also begin to get a feel of the places in our body where there is tightness, tension and discomfort. If we are sensitive enough to the energy force within us; we will begin to get a feel of the dark spots where we are experiencing resistance and where movement is not flowing smoothly.

'For instance you can easily tell if a man is out of balance and harmony by the way he holds his club. Watch the imperfections in his swing and in his manner of approach and you will immediately get a glimpse into his mood and his state of mind. However in saying this you must always remember to be mindful and humble. The key to this hole is not in judging and telling others where they are falling off centre; it is in paying attention and seeing it within yourself…and then correcting it.

'Through your swing here you will discover that it is in your body where you find all the previous baggage that you have inherited and are still carrying around within you. Golf can become your therapy couch and it will give you a sense of what it is you need to work through here in Earth school. Your body then serves as your curriculum as it reveals to you where the flow of Qi is stuck and it can teach you where imbalance and disharmony lies in your mind.

Indeed, metaphysicians over the years have been able to build up a whole field of knowledge that reveals to us the blind spots in our thinking and belief systems from the symptoms we create for ourselves in our body. Our bodies reveal perfectly to us the shadow places of unconsciousness that remain in our being.

'For instance, if we have problems in our digestion it suggests that we are struggling to assimilate some new piece of information; or struggling to adapt to changes in our circumstances. Stomach problems would be quite a common ailment for you to deal with on this second hole as you will no doubt be struggling to absorb and digest the powerful spiritual opening you received on the first. Indeed this may explain why western travellers go to India and experience mind-blowing states of consciousness... and the Delhi belly at one and the same time. However; you will be glad to know that the emphasis on turning from the centre and rotating the waist in the golf swing has already been enormously helpful for you on this hole in dealing with this potential health problem before it has even taken hold.

'So with this knowledge you can begin to feel the ways in which the movement of the golf swing helps to massage and loosen these tight and dark spots within. Through smoothing out your swing with your conscious attention, you can try to release the places where your Qi is stuck and not flowing and to bring your body back to a place of wholeness. This is all about grounding, absorbing, and integrating your spiritual opening down into the earth and healing the separation that still exists between spirit and matter. Through the way you swing your golf club you are really tending to your inner garden and becoming more conscious of where the weeds exist and how to help clear the space for life to continue emerging and flourishing there. In the first instance it is through your body that you must learn to work with your contract for incarnation here in Earth school and to hone yourself into a perfectly formed channel for grace to flow.'

'Can a movement practice like the golf swing really heal our bodies?' he asks incredulously.

'It is not about the miracle cure of healing your body from illness; but it is about removing those knots of emotional energy that are stored in the body and which in time can run amok and cause endless problems if you are not mindful of them. Golf is only one of many body awareness practices that can help untie these knots before they take hold and fester; but they are not the complete answer on their own. Just remember what I said about putting the pieces into the puzzle one at a time and that the second hole is just the beginning of a long road.'

'Even so it is still a bit hard to take in that just by consciously swinging this golf club more smoothly that I can help at all in fulfilling this grand commitment you've asked me to renew.'

'Well everything in this world is interconnected; scientists as well as mystics are now saying this is so. What this means in a nutshell is that if you are storing something toxic within the cells of your body then the whole of the world suffers for it. So rather than trying to change anyone else, or anything as abstract as the world; your first responsibility when living on this earth is towards your own physical and mental wellbeing. For it doesn't matter how grand a castle you build for yourself in this life or how many souls you try and save; if this responsibility is not taken care of then that castle will simply have no foundations.'

'So I have to recognise and honour this step before I can move on with my game?'

'That's absolutely right. Learning to swing your golf club in a smooth, balanced and harmonious rhythm will have a far bigger impact on your game than you might imagine. I promise that you will appreciate this more over the coming holes.'

With that made clear I sense that he is almost ready to complete the second hole. He will need to return back to this place many times again I am sure but for now I am confident that he has learned enough. I return the six iron back into the bag and I gesture for him to start walking on without a further word. When he finally approaches his third shot; he does so with many small practice swings as if getting a feel for the way the Qi is moving down through his body. He is getting a feel for where the emotional knots might be within and through his movements he is starting to consciously release them.

When he does strike the ball it falls on the green but doesn't bring the same graceful illumination as was given to him on the first hole. For a moment there is a flicker of disappointment etched across his face from being unable to recreate the magic here. But I need not intervene for the disappointment does not take hold of him as once it might. It does seem as if his stamina for the journey is building and he is not so discontent to take a further two putts on the green to sink the ball into the hole. Indeed, as he records a bogey five upon his scorecard, I can see that the demanding child from the first is finally beginning his journey of growing up.

Watching the Mouse Hole

Behind the transition from the heavenly high of the first to the ground of the earth on the second lies the next error that we must now work through together on this third hole. For in putting his focus solely on the body; he has yet to transform the influence of his mind. As we come towards the teeing area; I feel I must forewarn him of what is to come down here.

'From your experience of the second you have started to recognise the link between the thoughts in your mind and the bodily reality you create. Now through these bodywork practices you may be able to clear the weeds from the garden; but unless you begin to work with your mind as well they will only continue to reappear again and again. On this third hole it is time to go even deeper down and to begin to clear out the roots.'

'How can I do that?' he asks of me curiously.

'Play the shot first and then we will go from there,' is my only mysterious reply.

I know this third hole well; and I know the way it has been perfectly designed to help us reveal the thick and tangled roots that lie buried deep within his inner garden. At 165 yards, it is short in length and is a hole that appears welcoming at first glance. The flag sits invitingly in the middle of a large flat green that is only guarded by two small pot bunkers at the front. However, it is only I who knows that appearances can be truly deceiving.

He takes a mid-iron into his hand and takes a few practice swings as he continues to remember well the instruction from the second hole. But then, as he stands square in his approach to the ball, I see it happen; as it happens to all who come to this place in their game. A veil has fallen over his eyes and what seemed open and clear a moment ago has now been covered. Hastily, he tries to avoid what is coming down upon him by instinctively racing through his swing; and in so doing produces an awkward looking low hook shot that takes the ball swinging wildly away to the left. It is a shot that inevitably happens when the timing of the swing is rushed and the arms come flying through to strike the ball with far too much haste.

After watching carefully to see where the ball had descended in the deep rough, he is embarrassed to look across towards me and to acknowledge his error.

'Why did you suddenly rush your swing?' I ask kindly enough.

'I don't quite know,' he inevitably stutters in amazement as if puzzled and not at all sure as to what has just happened here.

'Well what was going on in your mind?' I ask as I try and cajole his memory along.

'I don't know,' comes back the answer again after a long moment's pause of reflection.

'Exactly,' I answer back emphatically; which I am sure leaves him only feeling more confused. 'Look, let me tell you what I saw from here. In your practice swing you were flowing through calm and smooth and nicely in your body. Your garden was free of weeds. But then, just as you were ready to take the shot, the root suddenly popped out another weed to throw you off balance. You rushed your shot because you were trying to outrun the weed that was slowly coming your way by hitting the ball before it could snare you. Sadly that isn't the right way to deal with it; as you can surely tell by the result of your shot.'

'Well what was the root of this weed?'

'Only a thought.'

'And what was the thought?'

'That's what I asked you!'

When I saw that he was not at all amused by my joking around; I began to explain a little more based on what I know of how things go around here.

'Look, ever since you crossed that threshold you have been enjoying the openness of the beginner's mind and you have been basking in the open spaces of the golf course. In these spaces the cords of the outside world have not been able to touch you and you have easily been able to free yourself from the day-to-day worries that once captured your attention and ruled your life. But now on this short and enclosed hole you are starting to feel a little more hemmed in, and we are beginning to touch upon the subtle desire to escape that has been present in you all along.'

'The desire to escape?' he repeats my words as if not quite understanding what I mean.

'Yes the desire to escape. Now what do you think you are trying to escape from?'

'I don't possibly know,' he answers with meek humbleness.

'Well allow me to explain to you then. Going back to the first hole what I saw was your desire to escape from the heaviness of earthly existence *around you* by becoming more spiritually conscious; and then on the second hole I saw your desire to escape from the heaviness of earthly existence that exists *inside of you* by becoming more physically conscious. But in feeling hemmed in here on the third hole you must realise that deep down at the root the very thing you desire to escape from lies within your own mind! And yet you struggle here because you know that such a desire can never be fulfilled. You know that you can surely never escape free from yourself!'

'Desiring to escape my own mind?' he asks again as if not at all sure whether he understands me correctly.

'Yes let me tell you that it is within your own mind that the seed of all this heaviness in your world is created. And you know what? As long as you walk this earth it will always be there with the

45

potential to snare you no matter what you do to outrun or outsmart it. There is nothing that I or this golf course can give to you to take that seed away.'

'So what can I do with this seed then if I can't escape from it?'

'Illuminate it.'

'Illuminate it?'

'Yes that's right; illuminate it. What that means is that you just have to be very vigilant so that the roots don't have any leeway to take hold in your garden. Through illumination you ensure that no stray thought can lead you mindlessly by the hand.'

'Is that all?' he responds; almost flippantly in tone.

'Yes that is all,' I respond sharply. 'But do you really know the full implications of what that responsibility brings? Let me say again that you create your own world with your mind. If you experience suffering, regardless of whether it be by the hand of nature or man, it is only because you yourself created it in a moment of mindless thought. That hook shot over there was a hell solely of your own making. You can blame no person and no circumstance for it happening to you anymore. You cannot hold God to account. Not only that but you can no longer play the cop out card of pretending that you don't know better because you know full well now that you do. And nor can you avoid this by playing the innocent victim and pretending that the weeds come of their own will; and for you to merely spend your days just trying to clean up a mess that in truth you've created.'

In the silence that follows I can immediately see that what I am asking is beginning to dawn upon him…and that the weight of responsibility does not sit comfortably.

'Wait a minute here. There are a million things going on within this golf course that have absolutely nothing to do with the way I go about swinging my golf club in the here and now. So how on earth can you say that I am responsible for it all?'

'Because what is in the whole is in the one. There is no separation; there is no line where your responsibility begins and ends. You either go on living in ignorance by saying none of it is yours; or you live in consciousness by recognising that all of it is yours. There is no other place to stand.'

'You'll have to give me a bit of time to get my head around that one,' he answers as if totally flummoxed by this non-dual teaching that I have lain down before him.

'You will be waiting for eternity to get your head around it... because time won't let you make any more sense of it,' I warn.

'But I just need something to grab a hold of here,' he pleads.

'Well what else are physicists beginning to conclude in their research that collaborates what mystics have been teaching for years?'

'I don't know,' he replies with a shake of his head.

'That consciousness is a force that creates and shapes matter,' I answer definitively.

'What this means is that this world that appears to you to be so solid, fixed and predetermined by other forces is then nothing more than an illusion and a dream conjured up by your own conscious mind. Ever since your arrival I've watched and seen how you've been busy trying to escape from that fixed and solid world because you believe it to be separate from you. You've believed that liberation could just be found by merely distancing and separating yourself out from things that you perceive are holding you back. You've falsely believed that out here we are merely going through a sieving out process to remove all the dross and to leave only the pure enlightened self behind.

But this is all an illusion and that hook shot over there serves as a reminder that you will have to carry your mind, and the world that it creates, around with you for the rest of your days. It simply can't be dismissed and sieved away down the drain. The potential of hell is here within you in each moment just as much as is the potential of heaven...and there is in truth no getting away from it.'

'But isn't there the possibility of ultimate enlightenment; of dwelling permanently here in the silent and spacious void of the eternal now?'

'We spoke of those who try to do so back on the first hole and who simply become un-tethered space cadets that become lost in this vast cosmos and lost in their memories. Let me remind you again that as long as you still have a physical existence on this earth; there is no possibility for ultimate liberation from the shadows of this world. Every moment of your life offers a choice of where you want to put your attention and enlightenment has to be a choice you make in every second of every day. This choice of enlightenment may become easier and even instinctive in nature for some; but whilst there is still breath in your body there is to be no happy retirement into the spacious void. Life will always pull you back into the constriction of this third hole if you try to cut loose completely. Your humble vigilance must remain true till the end. That is your responsibility.'

'I hate that word responsibility though. In my world it carries such a heavy undertone to it. When I hear it I think of a wrathful God in the sky wagging his finger and saying you should do this and you should do that. Or I think of my own peers who want me to live up to their expectations and who burden me with a list of things that I should be doing with my life. I thought I came out here to get away from all of that.'

'Your right but this is not the meaning of the word I am using here. Responsibility is simply to do with responding as fully and courageously as you can to each moment; without trying to escape or duck from it. It has nothing to do with a list of commands you 'should' be adhering to. Remember that responsibility must come from the heart within not the mind without.'

'Okay, it sounds fair enough that I at least try to respond to what is happening in my own life on this earth,' he concedes. 'But it sounds too much to ask me to take responsibility for other people's actions too.'

'But I'm not asking you to take responsibility for the shots that other people play! All I am saying is that when you see some-one hacking around the course; don't draw the line between you both by thinking that it can't happen to you - because the truth is that the seed of that action lies in you just as much as it lies in them. No matter how well practiced you are at this game; in these moments it is truly wise to stay humble and vigilant rather than judging from a mind of separation. Hard though it is to accept, this is true even with the wildest golfers that have graced this game – the Hitler's of this world - who seemed to spend all their life hacking around in the deepest rough. Knowing that all acts of evil begin with a mere compulsive thought is how you take responsibility for your game…and for the game as a whole.'

'But merely knowing that the seed is within me won't stop *them* from hitting the same bad shot next time?'

'You can't possibly know what difference you can make to the whole by taking responsibility for the one. You just have to play your part and to trust that it does.'

'It is a big ask though to expect me to play this part of vigilance and to be *that* mindful of the thoughts in my head. It seems impossible to face and to respond to every moment fully conscious.'

'This isn't an exam that you can pass or fail. You are human and at times you will succeed and at times you will falter. But accept your nature and come to me humble and I am sure to pick you up again if you fall.'

Such words of unconditional love are rare for him to hear in a world where the perfection of performance is everything and failure is abject. In hearing them he falls utterly silent in respect before me.

'So how do I try and keep the roots out of my garden?' he finally asks as he reveals his longing to at least come and give it a shot.

'You must first begin to realise that it is simply not enough for you to separate yourself from the roles and duties you once performed out there in the world – those false responsibilities as you would call them. Cutting those strings may have helped you across the threshold…but you must remember that the mind that created those strings in the first place still has its place within you and its power over you. It is time now for you to take on the real responsibility of mastering your own thoughts and to stop them from dictating the shape of your game. To achieve this you must learn to practice the art of detachment and to bring some spaciousness around your own compulsive thinking.'

'But how can I practice such an art?' he asks, his interest piqued a little by the idea.

'It is all about the practice of separating out who is the observer from what is the observed so that you no longer identify and remain completely entwined within the endless train of thought. It is all about coming back to the present moment rather than being carried away unconsciously on the back of that train.

'So you are really saying that who I am is not the thoughts I think,' he interjects.

'Exactly. There is the essential part of you that is simply not touched by thought and that has nothing to do with the storyline of your life. Remove all the labels of who you think you are and see what is left behind. You will see that this is the untouched jewel of your being. It is the authentic self you are here to realise and to build your life around.'

'So you want me to stop thinking altogether then in order to discover this jewel of my being?'

'I am not saying that at all. Unless you want to regress back to a vegetable state; thoughts will always pass your screen of awareness. You can't just turn them off! The answer lies in observing their passage without getting *hooked* on them. As you do this you will discover to your surprise that although these thoughts seem so real and lasting; that they will pass away just as quickly as they appeared. It is in letting them pass that you will get the roots out of your garden.'

'So let me get this perfectly clear. You are saying that a compulsive thought hooked me in and suddenly changed the shape of my game.'

'Yes that's right.'

'And it doesn't matter whether that thought is malicious or benign; or whether it relates to the shot I am playing in the moment or not. It still has that power over my game?'

'Obviously if you are having dark thoughts that draw your attention into the deepest rough rather than the hole you are aiming for then it is inevitable that this is the reality you will create. But benign distractive thoughts like the one you had also have the power to change the shape of your game. In truth it doesn't matter what the root of the weed looks like. A weed in your garden is still a weed.'

'This mind sounds like a monster,' he answers laughing. 'Is there a technique I can learn to help me catch these thoughts before they hook me in?'

'The only way is to stay mindfully alert as to what is happening within. Be like a cat watching a mouse hole so that thought has no place to slip out unnoticed. And if the mouse appears, just look at it clearly in the eye so to speak. Be the watcher. There is no need to chase after it because it is only in your detached observation that its power over you will diminish. Know that the lingering sense of powerlessness is the greatest cost of your unconscious attachment to thought as it causes you to do things that you do not mean to do and to say things that you do not mean to say. It was your powerless attachment to thought that led you to hit that random wild shot over there.'

'You make the mere act of thinking sound like the work of the devil! What is so wrong with it when our whole civilisation has been built upon it? Thinking helps us solve our problems and to make our world a better place. What can I possibly do without it!'

'Did the mindless thought that passed through your mind when you swung the club a moment ago help you play the game better?'

'Well…no,' he concedes in reply. 'But I still need to think

ahead about what shot I want to play do I not?'

'There's a big difference between directed and mindless thinking. There is nothing wrong with focusing your brain on something specific in order to respond to the situations that arise moment-by-moment. As I said; as long as you are on this earth your mental abilities are there to be used as an asset. It has its place in the grand scheme. But let me remind you that you only use this brain for a mere fraction of the thinking time that you indulge in. For the most part your thinking is stimulated by this strange phenomenon we call mind; the ghost in the machine that has no useful part to play in your life. It is this phenomenon that churns out all these random and repetitive thoughts which clutters up space and takes you away from what is really here now. You must exorcise the ghost if you really want to find the jewel of your being. For there can be no spacious, silent and eternal now in its company. There is no wisdom, truth or love in the shadow it casts.'

'But for what purpose does this mind serve then?'

'We entertain it purely for the sake of company. Deep inside you really don't like to entertain the virgin silence of the present moment and the jewel of your being is far too naked and raw to lay your eyes upon. This is why you distract yourself with stories of your past that has been and your future that is to come for they appear to be far more pleasant and safe to be around. It is why you cannot help but fill a room with clutter than keep it empty and spacious.'

He falls silent again which I take as a good sign that he is listening and finding some truth in what I say.

'So how do you suggest I go about keeping the room free of clutter?'

'On this third hole you first need something that will serve as an anchor to stop your attention from drifting away; you need an object of meditation.'

'Something to focus on you mean whilst I am playing the game?'

'If you like. Now if you take a look across many spiritual traditions you will see how the movement of breath in the body has long been elevated as the most suitable meditative object to focus your attention upon.'

'Why's that so?'

'Well there are many reasons. For some the breath is God's greatest and most tangible gift and the more you lavish it with your attention the more you are lavishing him. For others the breath is simply the source of life; it is the thread that connects us to this earth and to this life experience. To honour breath with attention is to honour our existence. For others still the breath leads us home to our deepest nature. By controlling our breathing we are brought back to our centre and are brought back to a place of harmony and balance. From this place everything else can follow suit in our body and minds and we become calmer and less stressed and overwhelmed by events. Not only this; but the breath resonates with the throat chakra which connects the head and the heart and brings balance between our intellect and our emotions; thus cultivating wisdom and compassion in our lives. So you can now perhaps begin to see why the breath is valued so highly in many cultures.'

'I see. But how does it serve as an object of meditation too?'

'For me the greatest asset of the breath is that it is not actually an object at all! It is fluid and formless which makes it most suitable for anchoring you in the void of the spacious, silent and eternal now. You must learn that the key to mindfulness practice is that it must not be heavy and rigid; it isn't about obedience training so that your brain remains eternally fixated upon something so that no stray thought can ever slip in to hook you. Mindfulness training is meant to be light, soft, gentle and relaxed; and the natural rhythm of the breath helps to keep it this way.'

'It sounds a great practice to experiment with. But how do you want me to work with my breath whilst out here on the course?'

'Let me show you,' I say taking the golf club from his hands in order to demonstrate something whilst swinging the club around and through in a golden arc. 'Now have you ever noticed that the whole movement of the full golf swing mirrors a swinging pendulum that moves in the same rhythmic cycle as your breath? You see, when I draw the club backwards on the backswing I am naturally breathing inwards. Then as the club rests horizontal to the ground at the very top of the backswing there is a moment's pause when it sits square to the target and which completes the cycle of the inward breath. Then as I pull the club down, through, and around I am naturally exhaling and completing the cycle of the out breath. So as well as being a body awareness practice, the movement of the golf swing can also become your anchor of meditation to help keep your attention in the moment.'

'So what should I be doing differently than what you taught me on the second?' he asks; intrigued by this new practice.

'I want you to start *breathing the swing* as well.'

'Breathing the swing?'

'Yes that's right. Forget the golf club and the game to begin with; and just close your eyes and try for yourself this conscious breathing. I promise that if you do so you will naturally discover that the rhythm becomes deeper and far steadier in its flow. A stray thought may arise in your mind as you do this but you will become so anchored in the rhythm of your breathing that it won't pull you off centre as easily as it once did. It won't hook you in like it once did.'

I watch as he puts my instruction into practice by closing his eyes and just breathing. When I sense that he is softening and in the rhythm of it I put a ball upon the tee peg and place the club in his hands.

'Now I want you to keep your eyes closed and just let the club swing back and forth naturally; to breathe the swing into action. Can you feel the difference from the tee shot you played before?'

'Well yes. My swing seems smoother,' he eventually replies after giving it a try.

'Exactly, and your timing of the shot will be a lot more

accurate for it,' I add. 'Now I want you to go ahead and play the shot again.'

After playing the shot I pulled a dozen or more balls out from the bag as I wanted him to truly get a feel for the teaching before moving on with our game. On the first it was important for us to keep moving through and to not remain static on the course; but here on the third, practice helps us to build our mindfulness for the holes ahead. Such is the distractive power of our own compulsive thinking that we need to develop a lot of mental discipline in order to stay present and awake rather than spinning off. Through this practice on the third he will soon discover that there are in fact lots of roots deep down in his garden waiting to grab his attention.

So with each shot I can feel that his mindfulness is becoming much more reliable and sustained. He has that steely eyed look of determination as if he is not going to let that mouse slip out of the hole unnoticed whilst on his watch. In response his swing is now flowing so much more smoothly and it is starting to show a much more dependable consistency within it. Through due diligence I can feel that his stamina is building and building for the holes ahead.

Of course, as with all the holes we have played, we will have to come back to this third hole many times I am sure. Depending on how stirred up and choppy our pond is, it can take many moons to bring the waters back to that quiet place of complete stillness and calm. It takes a while before mindfulness becomes second nature and for order to be restored within a once cluttered and untamed mind.

However, though there is still more to be gained from the practice, the danger on this third hole is that it can easily become an unhealthy obsession and he will remain stuck here. Like all things there must be balance and I am not asking him to become like a perfectly honed robot that can carry out my commands to the letter. I want him to be a complete golfer and not just a third-hole expert. We must move on then and go in search of where his first ball has fallen.

Fortunately for him it was easy to find and it was sitting atop the wisps of long grass in this deepest of rough. I left him to play his shot and went off to gather up all the other golf balls he has struck. I turned back to see him strike a straightforward and well-judged wedge onto the putting surface. From here it took two further strokes of the putter to bring the ball to rest into the cup. Another bogey was marked upon his scorecard and I am assured that he is ready now to move on to the fourth.

These Feet Were Made For Walking

We are moving through the training quickly now and the technique of becoming mindful of the breath has given him a useful anchor to help detach from the train of thought that once cast its spell over him. As a result his swing has become even more solid and dependable than before and he is slowly gaining a certain level of mastery over the thinking mind that once held dominion over him. It is by no means complete but it feels a bright beginning. Another piece has been placed into the puzzle and he is now ready for the next to be given.

Again it is a perfectly designed hole for this next teaching as this is the longest hole on the course and it will take three full shots to get close to the green and the flag. It is perfect because after teeing off and moving down the long fairway I can tell that the breathing technique we learned through the golf swing is not enough to sustain his focus and attention…and that his mind is already beginning to roam elsewhere. For as all golfers will soon discover; it is very challenging to maintain one's concentration of mind over the full duration of a four-hour round of golf when there is so much spaciousness for it to wander off into! On this longest of holes then I know that the golf swing will not provide him with enough of an anchor to sustain his mindfulness through it. He desperately needs another type of practice to help him rest more securely in a diligent state of presence.

'Stop!' I instruct long before we reach the place where his well struck tee shot has come to rest.

He turns with a jolt towards me as if drawn out of some day-dream reverie and then immediately feels the wave of guilt as if caught red-handed for his mindlessness. He stops and looks towards me; but cannot hold my eye.

'Fear not. You are hoping to transfer the teaching from the second and third holes to the fourth and I am simply showing to you that it cannot be transferred. You've done nothing wrong but you must be a willing student who wants to receive the full training in mindfulness. Don't pretend because you cannot hide yourself from me.'

'Tell me then what I must do,' he pleads innocently.

'It is not enough for you to create this separation in your practice and to only bring your mindful awareness in the moments that you feel you really need it – namely in the exact moment when you approach the golf ball. I see many who go to their one hour meditation class once a week and who foolishly pretend to themselves that this mindfulness training can sustain them for the remaining 167 hours right until the next class. Let me tell you now that if you want mindfulness to permeate all the way through your life you have to be willing to give it your all wherever you are and whatever you are doing.

'Do you see that your meditation practice here on the golf course is so much vaster than the time you spend striking your golf ball; much like your experience in the world is so much vaster than the time you may spend sat on the meditation cushion? If you approach your golf ball with your mind scattered elsewhere it will be very challenging for you to bring it back to a state of calm. And even if you can; there is little success to be gained from doing so. Maintaining a sense of poise and stable equilibrium right through-out your practice is critical. This is all essential training in becoming a well disciplined spiritual warrior.'

'So what can I do to help me become such a complete warrior?' he asks earnestly.

'Let me be clear that the first thing is that ethics precedes meditation. In training to be a warrior through the martial arts it is absolutely essential that you are clear in body and mind before you engage your opponent. The second thing is that meditation also precedes ethics. What this means is that if your mind is allowed to wander loose after the shot has been struck then you are not absorbing and integrating what you have just experienced into the core of your being. The benefits you receive through your practice are flittered away and your experience of mastery over your body and mind will remain like a flickering flame. Your mindfulness will contract and expand rather than remain steady.

'Now on the second and third holes you were well trained in the first teaching of ethics preceding meditation; of getting clear in body and mind before taking each shot. But here on this fourth hole you must train in the second teaching of meditation preceding ethics. In doing so you will close the circuit and ensure that your mindfulness will be sustained at all times. Ethics leads to meditation. Meditation leads to ethics. Ethics leads to meditation. And so your stamina will build and build.'

'Build for what?' he asks curiously and with a sudden worrisome thought of what it is that lies ahead beyond this fourth hole.

'To help you through the trials that are to come. But worry not for now about that and simply take the next step that lies here before you.'

'So how can I not let my mind go loose after the shot has been taken?'

'I will show to you the practice of walking meditation,' I answer directly.

Without saying a further word I begin to walk forwards to where his ball has come to rest and he is left following behind as if waiting for further instruction and probably wondering if he at least should be trying to mimic my movements.

We arrive at the place where his ball rests in the light rough on the right-hand side of the fairway. On this longest of holes I reckon that he still has a full three hundred and twenty yards to cover in order to reach the green that can be seen in the far distance ahead of us. He takes a long iron from his bag and begins to swing the club and to approach the ball in the right frame of body and mind. The ball is struck smoothly towards the middle of the fairway although it seems to carry no great distance upon its flight and it has little momentum upon landing. Before moving forwards I add to my instruction.

'Okay you've just had what I would call a brief meditative experience. It is a precious gift that sits in your hand and you need to hold it carefully and to not just cast it away before your next breath even passes through. One way of holding it is to pass it through from one footstep to the next until you reach the place of your next shot. Simply imagine that you are placing a thread down so that one shot can move seamlessly through onto the next.'

'Please tell me more about this?' he asks, intrigued by the teaching.

'It is no different to the practice you were given on the third hole only this time your breathing movement flows through each step you take from one shot to the next rather than just in the flow of the golf swing. The attention you give to the rhythmic movement of walking just becomes another anchor that can be used to stay mindfully present here in the now. Remember that out here on the golf course you will end up walking a good four or five miles during your game...even six if you are playing badly enough...and so walking meditation becomes a most suitable focus that can help you move more seamlessly through it.'

He takes on board my instruction; but he begins by stepping forward almost as if he is trying to walk for the first time. His focus is too forceful and controlling as he tries to impress me with his movements. As a result he walks unsteadily and with an unnatural gait and I cannot help but laugh.

He turns to me with a scowl.

'What did I say to you about trying to hide things from me,' I chirp across to him with a smile. He simply looks back at me crestfallen.

'Hey don't look so worried. Remember what I taught you on the third about mindfulness being a light, soft, gentle and relaxing practice. You simply don't have to go around with that straight and solemn face and with a stiff robotic pose. There is no need to walk around like this mindfulness business is serious heavy work! Do you see that because you were so rigid in your movement that it took only one little laugh to throw you right off balance!'

'So what should I be doing differently then?' he said with his mood still dark and heavy.

'Just stop trying so hard!'

He looks at me a little puzzled by what I am saying as if I am telling him one thing and then swiftly telling him another. He clearly needs a lot more cajoling down this hole.

'Look, those who understand the practice suggest that you try and put only 25% of your attention directly upon the object of your meditation…not 100% like you are trying to do. You only have to touch it very lightly with the tip of your mindfulness sword.'

This explanation, however, only seemed to leave him as bemused as before. We were now passing by the fairway bunker that was there to catch the stray ball from the one who strikes their drive far too eagerly down here. I put up my hand for him to stop and pulled a club from his bag before dropping down into the soft sand. I began to draw a circle with the club head before placing the club upright into the sand at the very centre of it.

'Okay, the golf club represents your object of meditation and in your practice you have to remember that it is always there to help bring you back to this central place whenever you find yourself drifting away. But although it is here as a focus to give you your bearings you don't have to tie yourself tightly around it with such a firm grip. You will need to build a lot more trust in yourself and in your practice so that you no longer need to prop yourself up against the baby walker that you are holding tightly onto.

'I know this is tough for you to understand because in your

world out there you are taught that there can be only success or failure. In your mind you are either anchored to the club...or you are completely lost. This is why you are still treating your practice as if I am here testing you and that you have to prove yourself by holding on tight in order to pass this mindfulness exam. It is your fear of failing that causes you to try so hard and yet I must tell you that out here you don't have to prove anything to me or anyone else.

'So ask yourself then how you would approach this practice if you knew that you could not fail?'

'But you just told me that it is important to not let the gift flitter away after each shot. Now you are telling me something completely different!'

'It is an ancient teaching that the one that holds tightly onto something is as likely to lose it as the one that tosses it away carelessly. I am simply trying to show to you the middle way of mindfulness of not being too tight and not being too loose. When I see you being too loose I will say to you tighten up. When I see you being too tight I will say to you loosen up. The teaching appears contradictory only because you are contradictory!'

The cutting response stung him into a brief moment of silence; but it didn't last for long before another question came forth.

'Okay so you want me to loosen up a little by putting only 25% attention on my breathing through my footsteps. Where then should I put the rest of my attention?'

'Stop it,' I respond angrily.

'Stop what?' he protests as if taken aback by the force of my reaction.

'Stop this calculating mind of yours that is busy trying to control the practice. Let me tell you that this alone is what bars you from the gate of this teaching. Yes such a mind may help you to follow the recipe instructions from a cookbook; but it won't get you any further on this golf course. So stop it right now.'

'But you were the one who gave the instruction?' he pleads limply.

'Yes I did…but you don't need to fill in the gaps. If I had wanted you to put the rest of your attention on something else then I would have given you that instruction with it. The fact I didn't tells you that there is no further instruction.'

He continues to look at me somewhat bemused as to what he is meant to do next and so I will have to relent and soften my tone if I am not to lose him completely here.

'What I am trying to say is that your mind is searching for another object but I am simply teaching you that the rest of your attention only needs to rest upon the empty spaciousness as represented by this circle I've drawn in the line of sand. There is simply nothing in there to fill the missing gap! That is exactly why I said to you before that the breath was a perfect object of meditation because it isn't really an object at all. Go on and tell me what you think happens when there is room in your awareness for both the object – the breath – and the spaciousness out of which the object appears? What happens when you can successfully balance yourself on that tightrope of not being too tight or too loose in your mindfulness practice?'

'I don't know,' he responds still unsure as to whether he is being tested here or not to go ahead and really speak his mind.

'What happens is that you naturally gain true perspective and the jewel of detachment will swiftly descend before your eyes. It is only in this place of balance that you gain dominion over your mind; and the beauty of it is that it can all happen without any effort or force on your part. Not only *can* it happen but it *must* happen this way. Mindfulness practice becomes like a graceful dance as you lightly touch your hand upon the object of your meditation. Very soon you will be gliding through from one shot to the next on gentle tiptoes and not through these clunky steps.'

A deep silence descends between us as we walk onwards to where his second shot lies. He is quietly absorbing the teaching that has been given and is beginning to go about the practice with a lot more poise and inner self assurance. I sense that his flickering flame of mindfulness is slowly becoming more steadied and constant and that his stamina is building for the challenges that are yet to come.

He comes to the ball, pulls the club from the bag, and approaches with a solid and centred stance. I no longer need to stand so close for he is oozing with a strong and powerful confidence here. Finally, finally he is beginning to stand alone freely poised in his own abiding presence. His eyes are turning inwards to that quiet place and he no longer seems to be striving so hard to prove himself to me or anyone else.

The wheel of mindfulness from the last three holes has become whole and it is turning and turning with a gathering momentum that is self supporting and self sustaining. The vibrations are building and so when he comes to play his next shot he is simply glowing with radiance. It is the confidence of one who has gained dominion over his own thoughts and who is not leaking energy away wastefully from his own system. As a result, the strike is so crisp and true that the ball simply flies right through the green and bounds delightfully through the boundary fence that hugs tightly to the back of the fourth hole. His zestfulness has caused him to strike his ball right out of bounds!

He looks up at me in horror at his error and then looks down at his club to see if he had somehow taken the wrong one from his bag. But he hadn't of course.

'Don't look so horrified by the result,' I reply cheerfully. 'I will show you how to harness that power in due course. For now simply rest in knowing that the fire of the spirit is well and truly alight within you. You must welcome it and keep it burning ablaze…and you must let it lead you deeper into this game,' I add mysteriously.

I take another ball from the bag and pass to him the seven iron in exchange for the five iron that he is holding in his hand. I stand back as he approaches the ball in the same manner. Again the strike is true and this time it drops down softly to nestle perfectly upon the putting surface about twenty feet shy of the flag.

We walk on again in silence and I sense that he is truly beginning to get a feel for the middle way I speak of as I watch the movement of his footsteps. Again it is another hole we will have to return to many times in order to master the practice but I feel confident that he is ready to at least test himself against the holes to come. We arrive on the putting surface and I take hold of the flag whilst he lines up his putt. It is evident that the magic that graced the first still has not returned as the putt slides by the right side of the hole and stops a couple of feet past. But I know that all this matters not for now as the second putt is sunk…and a double-bogey seven is recorded upon the scorecard.

As we leave behind the fourth green together I know we have already reached a significant milestone in his game. It is significant because we have now come to the far boundary of the golf course and we will now be turning back towards the clubhouse for the next five holes in order to reach our halfway mark. We had arrived then at the furthermost point from the distractions of the world he had left behind. In this quiet place on the course it is easy to recognise that elusive quality of detachment from the seducing swirl; and he has already touched upon the sacred gifts of spaciousness, silence and stillness.

His eyes cannot help but turn back and follow that lost ball across the boundary fence and into the great unknown from where he once came. I can tell that he longs to take a hop and a skip to join it because it is very tempting for him to take his leave. The veil between worlds is very thin here on the fourth and there seems to be very little holding him back from crossing over. Out here his worldly life is but a distant dream to him.

'Remember your promise,' I remind him gently as I point towards the one remaining thread that keeps him tethered to the earth.

'I remember,' he answers with a sigh as he slowly turns his head back around to face me.

'So you understand why you must now turn your eyes away from my kingdom and back towards the world again?'

'I understand that I have this part to play; but I can't say that I understand why I must continue,' he admits honestly.

'It is because you can't fulfil your promise from afar. Out here you have stepped completely out of the perpetuating cycle of madness that just pops out weeds right throughout your garden and you are no longer a mindless force for evil in the world. That is what the gift of detachment brings to your life. But you can't stop here for you must now go forth and to turn things around for the better.'

'What does that involve?'

'It involves you anchoring a new vision onto the earth. From the first green, I have already awakened in you the taste of a unique vibration; which is the special sounding note of my kingdom. This is a note that you now hold within; but it cannot be kept inside of you for safekeeping and you have to return now in order to share it with all you contact. It is by this sharing that you will turn things around.'

'But how do you want me to share what I have learned here so far?'

'By just simply being the living demonstration of that unique vibration.'

'Is that all?'

'Yes; but don't think it is as easy as it may sound. Over these next few holes you will be put through many different tests which will seek to throw you off balance from holding that note. Out here on the distant fourth green it is very easy to live a soulful life guided by me; but we now need to see how well you can manage it when the distractions of the world are closer at hand.'

'Closer at hand?'

'That's right. Have you not noticed that out here at the moment that the game really isn't very important to you? Take a look at your scorecard and see how two single bogeys and one double have been silently marked on your card without a flicker of interest since your grand opening par.'

'I guess I have been more focused on your teaching than my score,' he admits sheepishly.

'Yes and up to now my teaching has been more about the spaciousness than the form of golf; and it has been more about arriving fully here on the course. But how will you cope when my teaching starts to engage you more with the form than the spaciousness of golf? How well will you maintain your balance then?'

'Well the question is why do I have to? What does it matter if the game and my scorecard aren't very important to me?'

'Because I am telling you that it is only through the game and your scorecard that you can fulfil your promise on this earth! It is like asking why this earth bothers to go through the process of existing within this universe. But do you understand that space only exists for us when two or more objects exist to define it? What this means is that I need the construct of this game in order to make my teaching real within it. The game may be ultimately unimportant, but it does serve the purpose of helping you to illuminate the highest truth of creation from within it. It is why you were born onto the earth in the first place and it is why I have to work with you down here in this halfway house now. I simply can't teach you anything in the void that lies beyond the boundary fence and the fourth green is as close as you will get to it as long as you have work left to do. And don't even ask why it matters for you to be here illuminating the highest truth from within the confines of this game. Don't go there because your mind simply cannot answer such a profound question.'

'So you are telling me that the more the game becomes vivid and real; the more powerful the illumination can become?'

'That's exactly right. Out here the illumination is weak because your game is weak. But over the coming holes the illumination of truth will either grow stronger...or it will get more buried. Your test is to make sure it is the former and not the latter.'

'Can you tell me a bit more about these tests of the coming holes?' he asks a little more brightly.

'Pass me one of your clubs,' I instruct firmly as he stops abruptly and watches curiously as I suddenly drop down into the greenside bunker. Obediently he turns and pulls out a six iron from the bag and hands it down to me.

'Let me tell you that ahead lies four distinct tests of all you have learned so far.'

I begin to draw another circle in the sand and this time I break it down into four segments.

'Now these four tests are based upon the four elements of nature; fire, air, water and earth,' I say as I direct the club pointedly down in each quadrant. 'They are the four powers of this world that you must learn to recognise and work with in order to gain success through this game.

'The element of fire is to do with the Lord of Death and your fear of abandonment. Fire is a spiritual power that serves to destroy what has died and to create space for the new. It teaches you to ride the rollercoaster of change in your world without fearing what might be lost in the process. Moving on; the element of air is to do with the Lord of Truth and the fear of humiliation. Air is a mental power that serves to 'clear the air' so to speak of stagnant thought forms and beliefs. It teaches you to be more flexible and open in your mind and to let go where you may be holding on to something limiting and false. Next is the element of water and this is to do with the Lord of Equanimity and the fear of heartbreak. Water is an emotional power that serves to move you more sensitively through the terrain of your life and to develop a healthy relationship to pain and suffering. It teaches you to keep the heart open and to keep the pulse of life flowing through you; neither drowning in or damming the flow with your ever changing moods. Finally we have the element of earth which is to do with the Lord of Commitment and the fear of disappointment. Earth is a physical power that serves to keep you solid, firm and steadfast in the midst of a changing and uncertain world. It teaches you to remain loyal, honourable and zealous towards the commitments you make in your life.

'So let me say that the more you learn to gain mastery over these four Lords, and the fears they invoke, the more successful you will be in maintaining your state of mindfulness whilst going about your business in this game and in the world. Master these four Lords and you will become an unstoppable success at the game of golf...and the game of life.'

'But how can I possibly gain mastery over these four Lords?' he asks, struck with awe by the fierceness of my instruction.

'You will learn soon enough. But if you want a hint then I advise you to take a look east and see what your ancestors there tell you. Take a look at the ways the ancient Samurai treated their sword and you will see how I want you to hold your golf club. What I want is for you to have such mastery so that none of these four Lords, and their elemental powers, can cause your club to wobble even for an instant. Now you have already been learning these past three holes how to master your club whilst the conditions have been benign. It is time to see how well you can hold mastery over it when things get a little more testing.'

'And by doing so I will become the living demonstration of your laws?' he asks as if clarifying that he understands.

'Yes by gaining mastery over these four worldly elements you will reveal that there exists a higher power and force at work orchestrating things. Through your mastery, you will demonstrate the potency of self realisation in bringing about personal and planetary transformation.'

'I still don't understand why you think I am up to this! How can I possibly gain such a level of mastery in a world that has far more power and control over my life than I?' he responds pleading against my demanding nature.

'It is because you are not destined to stay here on the fourth. But let me encourage you upfront that there is no force on this earth that can resist the movement of an empowered soul who acts according to the higher law of Divine Order. You could even put

69

one thousand men in opposition but they will not succeed for truth is a force that cannot be touched by the hands of lesser men. Failure and resistance only arises from within a fearful mind because when an honourable fearless warrior serves to act wholeheartedly upon his master's orders; let me tell you that the seas do part for him. The miraculous is truly possible when the hand of Divine will is at work. You just have to go forth in faith.'

'But I have so far to go from where I am now,' he laments dejectedly.

'A journey of a thousand miles begins with a single step. The time has come to take that next step.'

I pass the club back to him and he takes a look at it for a moment as if unsure whether he is ready to receive it. Instinctively he knows the significance of my offering and I sense that some foreboding has just suddenly dawned upon him from what I said before.

Over the coming holes the illumination of truth will either grow stronger...or it will get more buried. Your test is to make sure it is the former and not the latter.

He knows that this is a big ask as many have taken the club before him and have failed to harness its power wisely. Human history is literally brimming with stories and legends of weak men and women who wielded a wobbling golf club upon the world and who only wreaked havoc and devastation in the process. History has taught him all too well that he is a part of a violent, wilful, competitive, vengeful, arrogant, greedy, and selfish species that time and time again have betrayed the trust of their maker in the way they manage the responsibility of holding dominion on this planet. For him; being human is just not in vogue right now.

And in the midst of his anguish: I am sure the irony is not lost on both of us that he only came through the gate and out onto the course to try and escape all the madness of humanity. And now here I am attempting to throw him right back into the epicentre of the wound.

'I am afraid of faltering,' he finally admits humbly as he continues to hesitate from taking the club from my hand. 'You have just helped unleash this tremendous force of power within me and I know that this means trouble because I can't trust myself to keep the ball in play anymore. I may go out into the deep rough and never return if I am not careful so please be wise and keep the club out of my hands.'

'There, there. Come now. I am here beside you and you cannot possibly go wrong when I am guiding your every step. Deep rough or not; there is no such thing as eternal damnation and this golf course is a safe playground for you to come and have a go. It has been designed for you to take a risk.'

'But are you not tired of us going astray in the way we handle our clubs? Will your love never cease?'

'Never.'

'I just wish that I had a role model though; to know that there is at least someone who has navigated his way safely through these four tests ahead. You speak fondly of the ancient Samurai but I personally can't think of anyone alive today who really has the wisdom to handle earthly power with the light of conscience. I just don't know anyone who has learned from these elements of nature on how it is to really be on this earth.'

'That is because you have to find that strength and courage inside; not in someone else. I have faith that you are ready. The question is; do you have faith in yourself?'

'Not yet I don't; but I am at least reassured that you have it in me,' he responds honestly after a moment's thought.

'So will you take the club then?'

'Do I really have a choice?'

'Well ultimately you don't,' I admit honestly. 'We both know that it isn't your destiny to stay stuck here on the fourth green in this safe and cosy off-planet cargo hold where you do neither good nor evil on this earth. The momentum is carrying you forward to make a difference...and surely it is too late now to stop it,' I add enticingly.

With a grave mood of acceptance then he takes the club in hand and begins to walk slowly forwards towards the fifth tee. After raking the bunker clean; I follow swiftly behind.

The Lord of Death

$\mathbf{A}$ lthough the four challenges can arise in any order; I know that we are to go through in the manner I spoke them and that we are to begin on this fifth hole with the element of fire. But before we can take another step it is my task to strike the match in order to reignite his interest again in the game.

'How much do you want to bet that you can make a par on this hole?' I ask provocatively.

He looks across in surprise at my question. Then he stands on the teeing area and looks down the hole before us as if mulling over the possibility.

'Look it is not a difficult hole,' I speak to reassure him with soothing words of temptation. I take the scorecard into my hand and show him the yardage. 'See it is only a short distance of 380 yards from here and there are no major obstacles ahead. What do you think? Are you up for the challenge?'

The hole was dog-legged as it twisted sharply around to the right; but it was true that there were no major hazards and the rough was light. With his newfound strength he should be able to cut right across the corner and a decent tee shot here would leave him with only a seven or eight iron to the flag. It is truly a tempting hole that encourages the player to come and attack the dog-leg with the will of fierce intent. We couldn't see the green from here but the map showed us that there were only a couple of small bunkers guarding the sides of the green to catch the wayward struck iron. But despite this he was still looking unsure as to what to make of my proposition.

'I don't know,' he stammers uncertainly.

'Okay, how about the loser of the bet buys the winner a drink at the nineteenth?'

'Sure,' he finally says. It is plain that he is only willing to shake my hand to humour me and that at the moment the last thing he cares about is whether he gets a par here or not. But as soon as the direction of this hole changes from north to east; I know that his inner compass will start to spin.

After shaking on it he goes ahead and pulls the driver out from his bag. He is now definitely going to go for the big shot rather than play it safe and so he stands there on the teeing area with a level of focus and intent that has suddenly been raised a notch. He is at risk of becoming too uptight on the tightrope of mindfulness but he manages to keep it together and to pull off a sweetly struck drive that sends the ball off in the right direction. It wobbled slightly away from the target but it clears the corner and finishes safely on the fairway with only 140 yards or so left to the putting surface.

He strides on confidently a foot ahead of me and I am left wondering whether he has already forgotten our serious conversation from the last green. Does he know that I have set him up and that his club will wobble if he is not vigilant here? For I can clearly see the tell tale sign from the fire of attraction that is swirling overhead from my ignited match; and I can see that it is already trying to lure and seduce him within its flame. It is hovering and waiting patiently for a moment of weakness; and if it spots it, it will surely dart through without hesitation. I can see it because I know this old nemesis well. Its presence, however, is not a sign that something has gone awry because it is only an examiner that I have sent to test how well he can dance with this powerful force. It is only a matter of time before that question will be answered…but I am quite certain that he will stumble here.

I watch all of this unfold silently from behind as he comes to his ball and prepares to approach his second shot. In remembering his overzealousness of the last he has taken an eight iron from the bag and his practice swing glides back and forth smoothly without a glitch. The eyes are keen and there is a graceful moment's pause as he weighs up the shot ahead. Eventually he pulls the club backwards like a well oiled trigger and swings down and through to strike the ball ever so sweetly. And there it is. Right there in the precise moment of impact of the club's sweet spot touching upon ball, a powerful sensation has arisen within and I watch as those seductive swirls immediately latch themselves upon it and go straight through the gate that has unconsciously been opened.

It was the sweetness that caused the gate to open because, without even needing the confirmation of his eyes, he knows purely from the feel of the shot that the ball has come down to rest only a few feet from the hole. It is an exhilarating feeling that is absolutely delicious to him.

He looks up at me with a smile of contented satisfaction…but I am alone in seeing the veil of suffering that hides within its warm glow. For having snuck through the gate those seductive swirls immediately set to work in massaging his ego. If I was a little concerned that he had forgotten me and my forewarning before; then I have to say that the alarm bells are now ringing loud. He turns away and starts to walk with a bounce in his step as he moves closer and closer to the green. As he does so he can see even more vividly where the ball has come to rest and his ego is properly feasting upon the deliciousness of the moment. He will surely not relinquish it easily now.

Not only is his mind feasting upon the memory of the delicious shot but it is also now feasting upon a sense of one-upmanship from the bet that he was now surely going to win. He has only a tiddly eight foot putt before him and he has two strikes in hand to get it into the hole! But lost in time, his mindfulness to the moment has been well and truly toppled. I for one remain confident that the bet is mine to win because I don't think that it will be long now before his golf club begins to wobble.

He pulls the putter out of his bag with the adrenaline pumping fast. Not content with a mere par he seems desperate to keep on this roll by sinking the birdie putt that was before him. For having now gotten a taste of the sweetly struck golf shot, he is desperately hungry for more and more. So as he stands there on the putting green the lesson of the fifth hole is present and clearly illuminated before him. But he has been blinded to it for the moment and his mind has drifted away to a future moment in time when that ball has dropped into the hole and has satisfied his craving. Now; striking the ball in this state of mind may or may not bring about the realisation of his desire, but any chance of success has surely faded now that the power of his consciousness has been taken away from the present moment. This trainee warrior has then succumbed to the dancing fire of temptation and has been sadly exposed.

And, as will so often happen, the craving leads to a tightening of the grip as the tension that has been created between the present and the future sends a feeling of nervous energy through his system. His poise has been knocked off balance and he will try too hard now to bring about the result he desires. I watch all this and see how the extra burst of adrenaline bursting down into the golf ball causes him to strike the shot far too firmly and he sends it shooting wildly a few feet past the hole.

'This green seems quicker than the others,' he mumbles mindlessly in surprise; not even realising the true cause. As he comes and stands over his fourth shot I can see his shoulders have sunk like a stone in water and his whole body begins to tighten up even more as he is now desperate to get that ball into the hole in order to give him a sense of welcome release. But in rushing right through the par putt in order to get somewhere other than where he is now; the ball is struck somewhat clumsily again to the side of the hole.

With his poise having already been vanquished; I myself knew that this outcome was inevitable even before he'd struck it. For the one who seeks the final fulfilment of his sense desire in the forms of the game will never truly find it and he may find himself stuck upon this fifth green for eternity just trying to get that damn ball into the hole! If he is not careful this fifth green will eventually descend into an extreme form of crazy golf with the hole suddenly disappearing and reappearing elsewhere upon its surface just as the ball is struck towards it! Such is the nature of this impermanent world…and such is the madness of a mind that tries to pin its location down so it may disappear into its depths and feast upon her for eternity! On this fifth green the hole has become like a mother's breast he longs to cling onto even after it has run dry. He has forgotten where his real sustenance comes from and his club has wobbled.

Before he tries to take his fifth shot it is finally time for me to step in and to bring this sorry drama to an end before it escalates into an epic saga. It is worth noting in passing that not a single word has passed between us since the fifth tee for I have stood back and simply allowed him to unravel like this before my eyes. This is all part of his examination.

'Wait a moment. Take a step back and have a look around you. Breathe deeply. Know that this too shall pass.'

I am doing everything I can to bring some detachment back into his game and to pull him back out of the fire. He is jolted and looks at me strangely as if having forgotten who I am. He has become so lost in the dream of form that he knows not whether he is awake or sleeping.

'What happened,' he speaks forlornly; although I know he is only rueing the bet that has evidently been lost. He knows not yet of the greater cost of his seduction.

'You've sold your soul for the price of a perfectly struck shot,' I warn him harshly.

'How can you say such a thing!' he protests in return.

'Because it's true,' I reply bluntly.

'But why do you think such a thing to be true!'

'Because I have just seen what has happened here. And you, evidently by your admission, have not.'

'Well tell me what you know then!' he demands exasperatedly.

'This is all to do with your innate survival instinct.'

'My what?'

'Your survival instinct,' I repeat. 'Do you ever notice that when your bodily senses perceive something to be good that you open yourself to receive that goodness. By contrast when your bodily senses perceive something to be bad you will repel and reject that badness instinctively. Now tell me; when you hit that sweet little iron shot back there you instantly knew that it felt good didn't you?'

'I did. But what's wrong with that…and what's that got to do with selling my soul?'

'There is absolutely nothing wrong with that! As I say it is a natural survival instinct. The problem lies not in the senses and the body; but only in your mind and in the way it handles the information that comes through the sensory gate.'

'Handles the information?'

'That's right. You were tempted by the boost you received from that sensation and subtly your mind was telling you a story that '*when this happened I received that.*' If the thing you receive feels good then your mind can get easily seduced and you may start to play your game with an agenda of trying to strike as many perfectly struck shots as possible. But that is not the wisest way to handle the information.'

'Well isn't that why I am out here for now? To try and play the game the best I can?' he says thinking back to what he had been told at the end of the fourth.

'That is your mind talking here and not your soul. Let me tell you straight that you will go no further in this game if you are so willing to abandon your soul in return for the gratification of the next sweet shot. No further.'

'Hang on a minute here. You were the one who placed the bet

and who told me that I have to get interested in my scorecard again!'

'Remember what I keep telling you about the middle way. This is the way you must find if you wish to complete this hole.'

'What are you trying to teach me here?' he reacts angrily at my refusal to give it all to him on a plate.

'What I am teaching is that you are mistakenly assuming that the perfectly struck shot is an indication that you are on the right path with your practice and you assume that if you give more time to your game that you will receive more perfect shots in return and will play better golf. But these agendas are created in the mind and do not reflect the true nature of the soul journey we are on together. Success rests in the state of consciousness you bring *to this present moment* and cannot be found in the circumstances themselves. Success can only truly be found when you release these mind-made agendas altogether.'

'But if that is so then why did you place the bet?' he asks insistently.

'In order to teach you this valuable lesson! Do you see the irony that it was your agenda that cost you your success in the shape of these two missed putts? Now, if you had of managed to stay firmly present and had not held on so tight to the boost you received from the second shot; then I am certain that the promise of a drink would have come to you like a sweet forgotten surprise.'

'So am I not to enjoy the golf shots I strike?'

'You can enjoy them in the moment; but only in that moment. Then you must let them go in order to meet the next new moment afresh. Let the guest come into your home but don't allow him to linger.'

'Even if the guest is my best friend?' he asks thinking back to the glory of his second shot.

'Especially then,' I reply insistently. 'Now this is all part of your training in becoming a real warrior in this world. The mature warrior is the one who does not give his power away to any outer situation and he is the one who maintains a vigilant guard over his senses so that he is no longer seduced off balance. He is the one who is no longer tempted to sell his soul for temporary pleasures. He is the one whose club does not wobble under the weight of temptation. And he is the one who knows the illusory nature of perceptive experience.'

'So you want me to just override what my survival instincts are telling me then?'

'No absolutely not! Keep remembering the middle way I tell you about by taking heed of the information that comes through your senses…but of not letting it dictate your game. Never strike the ball from a place of hunger and with the hope that a sweet shot can fill some vacant hole in your life. Don't give the game a power that it can't have over you.'

My words sink in but his face reveals a look of confusion.

'But was I not the one who came out here on the course starving and who received a blessing of grace back on that first hole which came and filled my cup to the brim. If I don't play hungry then how will I ever have room to receive that again?'

His question sounds a wise one; but I know that its direction is sadly misguided.

'Do not confuse with what was given to you on the fringes of the first green and what was given to you here when you played that sweetest of iron shots back there. What happened on the first was indeed a revelation but you must understand that this arose from beyond the forms and objects of the game. It never touched upon your five senses and the scrutinising mind behind it but went right through the locus of your sixth sense. It was an experience that had the power of addiction, but not of seduction, because there wasn't an enticing dance taking place between you and the game. On the first hole there were no objects to seduce…and no self to be seduced either. There was also no starving self who was desperate to receive the gift of the perfect shot; and likewise there was no overindulged self that had to relinquish it.'

'So you are saying my hunger in the beginning was just an illusion?'

'No. What I am saying is that the hunger of the first is the only thing that is real. This hunger on the fifth is the illusion. The difference is that on the first you knew that your hunger could never be satiated by a delightful five-sensory experience, would not be satiated by a mere sweet golf shot; whereas now on the fifth hole you wrongly think it can. But it isn't called a *sweet shot* for nothing! For on the first it is rightly the dessert that just tops off a hearty meal; whereas on the fifth you've now foolishly turned it into the main dish of a one-course dinner!'

'But both experiences felt the same to me! How can you be so sure?'

'Really are you sure you haven't forgotten what was given to you on the first? Then you didn't want to get the ball in the hole at all and now on the fifth you want to sink it as soon as possible! Then the golf you were playing was so insignificant and now you are so uptight about it! On the first you were hungry for truth and now you are merely hungry for pleasure. And you wonder why I think you've sold your soul.'

'But how can I tell the difference between the two in foresight and not in hindsight like this?' he asks a little more humbly now.

'Only by knowing thyself intimately,' I answer definitively. But he only looks at me blankly in response.

'You have to know how your mind ticks,' I say continuing on but still only getting a blank look back at me. 'Look, what I am telling you is that the delicious experience of that iron shot was only received through the locus of your five senses. Now which sense is the most dominant of the five in golf?'

'The sense of touch?' he finally deduces after a long moment of consideration.

'Correct. And it is through the practice and experience of hitting many eight iron shots that you can begin to distinguish between the different sensations that come through this gate and to understand what they mean. Through time you can build up a massive storehouse of information in your mind where every sensation of touch is neatly categorised along a scale of good and bad. But then in the very midst of all of this sorting and processing of information from your interaction with the game; a sudden spontaneous experience arises which you just know is utterly unique and which has no place to be boxed away in your mind's ordered system. It is as if it has suddenly just landed plonk in the middle of the storehouse without coming in the gate like everything else; and the mind just doesn't know how to process it. When these revelatory moments happen, like on the first, they don't slink and hide away in the corners; they come to stare you right in the face. They are not subtle; they are momentous.'

'But what has this to do with knowing thyself?'

'Well if the storehouse is empty, or if it is full and you're not at all aware of how it operates, then the moment of revelation isn't going to stand out for you is it? What I am saying is that you have to know first what can be boxed away in order to recognise what can't.'

As I speak these words I notice him suddenly becoming excitable as if a switch has just been turned on from the recesses within.

'Yes, yes, in hearing you say this I feel I *can* taste that again now from the first…and your right it was completely different! My body is just tingling again with the sensation of it now that I am feeling it! How could I have forgotten so quickly!'

But as swiftly as the light comes on; it grows dim again as his mind wracks to get a grip of this hole and its teaching.

'So what you are saying then is that by being more vigilant of what is going on in my mind's storehouse that I am suddenly going to recognise and savour more revelations like the one I had on the first?'

'No. Just forget about mystical revelation for now. In truth it doesn't matter whether you are standing vigilant at the front gate of your senses or not; for divine revelation will find its own way through. Being vigilant does nothing in itself to improve your chances of grace coming to visit your life. All I am really concerned about here on this fifth hole is finding out how well you can maintain order in your home *once the guest has already come inside*. When it comes down to it do you stand back and allow him to take the best seat in the house; or can you be firm and hold that seat vacant for the most exalted guest who might one day come to visit?'

He falls silent for a long drawn out moment which is a good sign that he understands my metaphor; and understands who the most exalted guest is.

'Please tell me more about the teaching of this hole.'

'Do you remember what I said to you about the four elements?'

'Yes.'

'Well this hole represents the element of fire which is to do with temptation and seduction. Now ultimately it is your fear of abandonment in the nakedness of the present moment that causes you to clothe yourself in your memories of the past and your hopes for the future. It is your fear of abandonment that causes that roving eye of yours to both hold on to the good you have and to chase after the good you desire. But this hunger only adds more fuel to the fire until its force overwhelms you.'

'Abandoned by whom?'

'By anything in this world that you currently hold dear. You fear that the fires of this world, those sweet eight iron shots that have long kept you safe and warm, will go out on you and will leave you cold and alone. That is why you are so eager to bury them in the hole here for safekeeping before you lose the memory of them or before they are tainted with a countering bad experience. It feels raw and scary to let go and to be in this state of not knowing here in the present; but this is the only real place for a warrior to be.'

'So what can I do to overcome these fears?'

'Simply know that nothing in this world is permanent and enduring. At some point in time this golf course and the world it represents will be gone from you. There will be no golf clubs, no golf balls, and no little holes carved in the landscape for you to play with. There will be no you to play the game either.'

'Well I don't know how thinking about all of that helps me!'

'Fear has no place in reality; it only lurks in the realm of illusion. The Lord of Death is only a phantom that comes by night. Illuminate what is real and he has nowhere left to hide.'

'So you want me to put the fire out then by pouring the cold water of reality on it?'

'No; not at all! All you have to do is to remember what I say to you about finding the middle way. The one who chooses to let the fire go out is the one who becomes cold and impotent with no blood in his veins. His golf club goes limp and there is no zeal in his grip. He is the one living on the sidelines of his life; the one who refuses to go further than the fourth green. It is no random co-incidence that live and evil are words that are so intertwined for the reward of living your life on this earth inevitably carries the risk of getting burned in its heat.'

'So even though the fire draws out the phantom; you are still saying it is a good thing?'

'Yes for it is the fire that alchemises the base metal into gold. So when the club strikes the ball on impact you must be willing to embrace the energy that is released in that moment; to live in the warm ecstasy of that moment; to be transformed in that moment. That energy is your fuel for fulfilling your purpose on this earth. Now can you imagine if we lived without this fire in a static and permanent world where nothing changed and where there was no death or loss?'

'Well it certainly would be a very safe and secure world,' he answers instinctively.

'Yes but not a very stimulating one either for nothing new would emerge or grow in such a world. Without death there can be no life and without loss there can be nothing gained. Do you remember what I said on the fourth that without form there can be no space? Well likewise without change there can be no revelation. Let me tell that it was the power of the fire, and the fire alone, that drove you through the gate and onto this journey of self discovery and self realisation.'

'I just have to be careful then in how I channel the energy on this journey of mine.'

'Yes, as I said before; *let it in but do not let it linger.* Use it but do not be used by it. Always remember who the special guest is in your home and make sure he holds the exalted seat for he is the only one who can satisfy your hunger. Never forget what is true for what is false.'

'But how will I know if the phantom has outstayed its welcome?'

'You will soon know by the way your club wobbles like it has done on this fifth green. With enough awareness it really isn't hard to spot when you have been seduced by the illusions of sense experience and have forgotten what is ultimately real.'

'And how will I know if I've shut the door on him too soon?'

'Again with enough awareness you will see the fire go out whenever your grip goes limp and your club wobbles in that way. Trust me; you will know when you have lost all your intensity and passion for the game.'

'But I still don't understand why I must find and walk this tightrope!'

'It is all part of your preparation of what is to come. Your maker needs to know how well you can handle these elemental forces of power before he can trust that you are a reliable vessel for him to work in and through. He needs to see that your club won't wobble before greater responsibilities are placed upon your shoulders later in your game.'

With a nod of the head the teaching has been received and he stands there alone for a moment without movement as if he is slowly closing back the gate of his senses and waving the seductive swirls away from his home. Finally he opens his eyes and is ready to take the short putt that lies before him. Now that he is firmly back in the nakedness of the present moment; the ball is struck confidently into the hole.

The Lord of Truth

As we walk silently away from the fifth green together I'm all too aware that this game consists of a natural flow of ups and downs. The key to the fifth hole lay in moving gracefully through the up movement and not holding on tightly to it. I know all too well that it takes a lot of inner self assurance and confidence for someone to be free of attachment from the circumstances of their lives and to not depend on the energy they receive from the pleasant experiences they enjoy. It takes a lot of wisdom and a keen discernment to be able to step away from the dance before it spirals out of control.

But he is showing welcome signs of progress and I feel confident that he is ready to move forwards to the next challenge. I know that here he is going to have to find a way to work with the opposing down movement in his game...and to not hold on too tightly to that either. It is time then for him to work with the element of air.

The down movement arises then with a change in the weather and on cue a keen wind begins to gust strongly into our faces. The seasoned golfer knows this old nemesis well and he inevitably shrinks in its presence for it is not a welcome one to him. Put that golfer on a course with calm and benign conditions and his spirit will soon begin to soar as he can go about his practice with ease and self assurance. However, put that same golfer on a course with a fowl wind and you will soon see him crumble under the weight of his difficulties. The wind is a nagging force that whispers menacingly into the golfer's ear that the game is going to get a lot harder from now on.

On the golf course the wind becomes a most apt symbol for the difficult situations and difficult people in our lives that we would normally wish to avoid but which ultimately can become our greatest teachers. And adding to the sense of difficulty was the fact that this was the second longest hole on the course; a tough 520 yard par five that stretched out along a gentle uphill slope to a flag that could barely be seen in the distance. The wind coming briskly into our face simply added another fifty yards to the hole in an instant. And not only was it blowing against him; it was also gusting across crossways. This crosswind would make it very tricky to navigate the ball safely down a narrow fairway that had dangerously thick rushes on either side that were waiting to gobble up the errant strike.

In looking across at my student I can see his shoulders drop even before he has taken the club and stepped forward upon the tee. One look down this long and demanding hole was enough for his mind to tell him; *there's nothing for me here…get me out of there fast!* I could even stand and watch the defences being raised for his mind knew in an instant that this hole spelt trouble; big, big trouble. I watched his eyes become cloudy and his spirit swiftly depart the body with the mind's letter of permission in its hand. The lights have gone out and all that is left behind is an empty spiritless shell; a body that has been left to fend for itself.

So after a momentary respite from his troubles on the fifth green; he has rapidly dropped back and disappeared into a state of survival mode where his only bodily choice is to either fight this nemesis or to flight from its grasp. How little does he know that there is a much truer response yet to be found.

I watch all of this happen and I see that he hasn't been able to transfer the teaching of the fifth across to the sixth. He is still not ready to stand true in the present moment regardless of the circumstances around him. His golf club is wobbling again even before he has begun.

So he stands alone on the tee with gritted teeth and it looks as if his bodily instinct is pushing him to put up a fight with the elements. He does so by changing his swing to conquer and wrestle with the change of weather. I watch as he starts to swing the club a little harder and he tries to lower the trajectory of his shot by placing the ball in line with his back rather than the front foot. But though these skilful changes bring some success; the ball he strikes doesn't seem to flow as smoothly off the club head as when he was swinging more naturally and smoothly. His timing has gone awry, and though the ball has landed safely in the light rough at the fairway's left hand edge; it has travelled barely 180 yards forward.

The outcome of the shot is instantly met with a frustrated grimace lined across his face. He begins to stomp off in annoyance that this hole is going to be one long drag and he seems desperate to get it over with as quickly as possible. I could stop him here; but again I know that I must step back and allow the process to unfold along its own course.

The ball was resting down and was certainly not lying in a position to attack with force. But, ignoring the facts of the situation, he recklessly pulls out the three-wood from his bag and begins to take a few wild practice swings. He is desperate to try and make up lost ground and to get 'this damn hole over with' as soon as possible. In his hotheadedness he has lost all sense of wise discernment and poise of movement.

Inevitably the shot is taken without any timing again as flailing arms and flying tufts of grass mishmash together on impact; sending the ball flying off low, and askew to the right, where it finishes in the rough on the other side. It comes to rest barely 100 yards further ahead. He looks up to the heavens with an air of resignation and his shoulders immediately droop again. It seems as if the strong headwind has now gnawed away completely at any lingering resistance. He has cast down the judgment that there is *definitely* nothing left for him here on this hole and that he must now place steel around his heart in order to protect it from further misery and pain. The letter of permission for the spirit to take a temporary leave of absence has been extended to a more permanent arrangement on this sixth hole. Left to his own devices I am sure he will happily go through the motions of completing the hole out of a sense of polite duty; but he will no longer dare to engage with it by the power of his heart and soul. He has become completely absent to himself.

Before he even takes another step I know that it is time for me to come forward and to put my arm around his shoulders.

'Be not afraid. It is safe for you to be here,' I speak reassuringly.

He looks up and is startled by my words for he is completely unaware of what is happening here.

'What?' he stutters back as if not wanting to be seen in his absence.

'Where have you gone to?' I throw the question back at him as if sending out the flash of my torchlight into his empty home.

'I am here,' he answers defiantly but without truth.

'Can you remember what I taught you on the fifth hole about those honed survival instincts of yours?'

'Yes. You said something like when I feel something is good that I've learned to welcome it and when something feels bad I've learned to reject it.'

'So can you look and tell me honestly whether you have rejected this hole because of this wind that is blowing down here?'

He is silent for a moment as he simmers over the question.

'Well probably; I guess,' he finally offers reluctantly in return.

'Then how can you be truly here in this moment if you have rejected it?'

'Well tell me what you want me to do then!' he answers boiling over in fury.

'As I said to you; to be not afraid and to know that it is safe to be here.'

'So you are telling me again that you want me to go against my own survival instincts!' he answers exasperatedly.

'No. I never said that on the fifth and I'm not saying it here. What I said then, and what I say now is for you to remember again the middle way and to stop speaking of these extremes of either/or.'

'So what is the middle way here then?'

'It is the path of acceptance and non-resistance.'

'Then go ahead and teach me this way,' he answers tetchily.

'I will but first let me explain to you a little bit more about the system of reasonable justice that your mind operates by.'

'System of reasonable justice?' he repeats confusedly.

'Yes. This is a system that is built upon rules of fairness where good actions deserve good consequences and where bad actions deserve bad consequences. It is a system that has been devised by the hands of men to bring about a reasonable sense of order and control over the civilised world and it is a system that is also inherited deep within your own mind. Now what is it that drives the civilised man to create such a scheme of earthly justice?'

'I don't possibly know.'

'It is a protective mechanism that shields his fear of humiliation.'

'Ah this is the second fear you mentioned,' he answers perking up.

'Yes that's right. No man will dare to expose himself in this world unless he is certain that he will not be humiliated by the circumstances around him. Now he knows instinctively that the only way to create this certainty in his mind is to feel that he is in complete control of his affairs. Deep in his mind, and deep in your mind, is then a hopeful belief that if one plays fair by this set of rules that one will be protected from these experiences of humiliation.'

'I see. But how does this relate to what is happening here on this sixth hole?'

'I am quite sure that you can see how this scheme of earthly justice has been set up here on the golf course. The fairway and the green rewards the good shot whereas the deep rough is the punishment that awaits the one who is wayward. The scorecard too is a record of one's life measured against the recommended par score that one should be striving towards. Out here there is a list of seventy-two commandments of where you should and should not be on the course. Fairway, green, putt, putt, fairway, green, putt, putt... and so on. And even though the handicap system is in place to help give the novice golfer more leeway for error...there are in truth very few golfers who are truly content to play their game to handicap once they've had the taste of the 'perfectly' played hole.

So day in and day out you come out here in earnest as you practice and practice in order to be able to meet the standards. And what drives it all is the hope that one day you can stride out on the course without any fears of humiliation haunting over you. You hope that one day in the future you will be able to come out here knowing that you are in complete control over your game and to be able to open your heart fully within it. Now the standards may be more exacting out here; but the desire for predictability, certainty and control remains the same. We all play the game with the desire for a guaranteed outcome from every shot we take.'

'And so what is wrong with this earthly scheme of justice and this drive for perfection?'

'The sad irony is that such guarantees are impossible to be fulfilled and so you will never release yourself from your fears by taking this path. It won't lead you to a promised land where you can walk freely with an open heart. What a funny paradox it is that this scheme has been setup to protect you from abject humiliation; and yet ends up keeping you bound in the fear of it anyway. For despite your best efforts to control your ball; out here on the golf course there is always a loose shot or a fowl wind awaiting somewhere and this is the fear that hangs over all who play the game. It matters not whether you are a beginner or a seasoned player; the truth is that the wind will come and sweep through your game regardless. The wind comes to level the playing field and even the most enlightened masters have to go through the humiliating pains of birth, sickness, old age and death. The difference between beginner and master cannot then be found in the level of control they have over their golf ball; but can only be found in the response to these trials when they come.'

'So why do we even bother to play then if we know that the game will only humiliate us at some point in time?'

'It is a wise question to ask why the golfer is compelled to play out this masochistic act and to bear all of this inevitable pain of human experience again and again. I have heard it said before that life is like taking a boat out to sea that is going to sink. Why do we do it? Why do we bother to perform the script that has been given when it only leads us to tragedy at some point along the way? I cannot possibly give you a reasonable answer to such a question and you will have to contemplate deeply upon it. My only business is to help you through the journey as successfully as is possible. My business is to make sure your club doesn't wobble along the way.'

'So how can I successfully get through this trial of humiliation then?'

'Do you remember what I said to you on the fifth about fear?'

'Vaguely,' he responds. 'But please remind me again?'

'What I said was that fear has no place in reality. Face and illuminate what is real and you will find it has nowhere to hide.'

'And how do I do that?'

'As I said to you; only through the middle way of acceptance and non-resistance. To do this you need humility and a strong dose of humour.'

'In what way will they help me illuminate what is real here?'

'Well in your conceited arrogance you believe that the wind is here as an affront to your scheme of justice. In vengeance you shake your fist at your God in heaven and demand to know why you have been forsaken. You demand a reason from him for coming out here and playing this game and you demand to know why the wind comes to take your ball off course. You demand to know why you end up where only sinners are meant to go when you've been such a good little boy at playing by the rules. When the wind blows you stubbornly refuse to come out and play anymore because the game has descended into a lottery; a random game of chance.

But in truth the wind is simply here to highlight the illusion you hold about having complete control over the outcome of your game. The wind is simply here to humble you into seeing what is real and what is false.'

'And humour?'

'Well it was literary figures like Dante and Shakespeare who showed us that tragedy and comedy are simply two sides of the same coin. It all depends on how you look at what is happening here as to whether you are going to cry in your lament or laugh at the mysterious ways of divine play at work.'

'But why must it be this way?'

'Because if you arrogantly assume that you must be in complete control of your affairs then you will not be of any use to your maker because you will not easily accept your place on the stage and away from the Director's chair.'

'I see. So he humiliates me to put me back in my place,' he answers, still unconvinced as to whether he really wants to put his faith and trust in such a seemingly malignant force. 'How can I begin to put this teaching into practice in my game?' he adds.

'The first step is to know humbly what is in your hands and what is not.'

I drop a ball to the ground and take a five iron from his bag in order to show him.

'Now let me tell you that all that is in your hands is your approach to the ball and the movement of your swing until the precise moment of impact. Where the ball goes from the moment of impact is simply none of your concern and all you are to do is to play the shot before you as best you can. Now on the first few holes of our game you learned how to handle the power that lies in your hands and I must remind you that the purpose of these tests is to see how well you can continue to hold it in trying circumstances. But sadly, when you arrogantly took out that three wood from the bag and took that swipe at the ball, you gave your power away because you were unwilling to be humble and to accept the moment completely. In your mind you were lamenting where you should be on the course and you tried to do everything you thought you could do in order to get back on track.

'But in truth the ones who are humble are the ones who have all the power in this world because they are the ones who don't try to be somewhere other than where they are *now*. They are the ones who have the stamina to get through this hole and for this reason alone they are the ones who are most effectively used as channels for grace.'

With that I stand and swing the club to send the five iron away sweetly down the fairway.

'The key instruction is to never give away your timing in your swing,' I add definitively.

'But should I not take account of the wind in my approach?'

'Of course you take account; but never, never, never give away your timing to it.'

'Where does acceptance and non-resistance come in?'

'It is all about releasing those expectations that life should be any different to what it is right now. It is about a deep, humble and trusting acceptance in the moment that you are in the right place at the right time no matter the circumstances. It is about holding a basic openness to this experience that has no fear of what the wind might do. It is about the knowledge that regardless of whether it takes your ball deep in the rough, or causes it to fall short, that it doesn't have the power to name who you truly are. Remember then that you are not the script that you are performing and it doesn't have the power to humiliate you like your mind would have you believe. You think that your maker humiliates to put *you* back in your place; but, beyond appearances, that is not really you who is being humiliated at all. It is merely a false pretender to your throne. So deep down, even though we play the game with the passion to perfect it; we don't in truth *mind what happens* because we no longer kid ourselves that we need to pencil in the happy ending first. It is about letting go and being playfully light and humorous regardless of whether you find yourself on the fairway or deep in the rough. This game will only send you mad otherwise.'

'So please remind me what element we are working with here?'

'This is the element of air. Air is the breath of the divine coming to bring life to the stage and to bring all that this entails from ecstasy to tragedy and all that lies in between. It tells the evolving and changing story of creation in all of its unpredictability and uncertainty and in all of its complexity and in all of its contradictions. To embrace the element of air is to be willing to embrace the black of tragedy in our lives and to grow stronger through our trials. In embracing this element we no longer hold on so rigidly to our pure and straight line sense of reasonable justice of what we think is right and wrong. The free flowing air blows through to teach us that life is just too big to be pinned down by the petty mind schemes we put in place. It comes and blows a big raspberry in our face whenever we get puffed up and self righteous in our minds.'

'And what does this element teach me in my training as a warrior here?'

'It teaches you to be adaptable and flexible to the moment rather than being so rigid and uptight. It teaches you to never get stuck in a set pattern of thinking, believing and living in the world so that when change comes you can bend rather than break with it. It teaches you to soften any false pride and arrogance that may arise when the conditions are benign and when the ball seems easy to direct and control.'

He falls quiet as he absorbs the teaching and we begin to walk to where his ball has come to rest. I can see his focus becoming more intent towards the ball and its current position. He is beginning to accept that this is the shot that he has to play and he is slowly letting go of all those judgments that tell him that he should not be here at this moment in his game and that he needs to get somewhere else. His ball is lying down in the rough and so after a moment's contemplation he discerns the right club to take for the shot at hand – a nine iron – and repeats my instruction like a mantra in order to maintain his poise over the club in his hand.

'Please don't let me give away my timing. Please don't let me give away my timing.'

The strike is a true one and there is a warm feeling of peace that has descended upon him because of it. He is beginning to find the right way through this most exacting of trials.

The rest of the hole pans out like a dream as he takes a long-iron for his fourth shot and through a generous act of grace it sails true onto the green. He even successfully gave the right allowance for the cross-wind from the right. Naturally, even though we can't control its destiny, we do discover that the flight of the ball will tend to mirror the state of the mind...and the truer the mind the truer the shot will be. But this will be a teaching for another hole. For now he can simply bask in the glory of his acceptance. Although his ball rests on the green it is a good thirty feet from the hole. This time though he manages to take two steady putts to coax the ball into the hole and he can record a well-earned bogey six upon his scorecard.

The Lord of Equanimity

Having safely navigated his way through the long and arduous sixth hole I can see that he is ready to catch his breath again. Already he can see that the seventh hole looks a lot more inviting ahead of him; indeed it is a 170 yard par-three that slopes down steeply to the green below our feet. A bank of tall trees lie in a semicircle around three sides of the green and they stand as protective sentinels who will gobble up the wayward or overeager strike. However there are no obstacles at the front for him to worry himself over and it really is a spacious and accessible green to approach. And now the sixth is complete; the wind has eased back to nothing. The calm benignity of this moment clearly leaves him with a warm feeling of respite.

I am not so complacent though as I for one can see the subtle wound that remains unhealed from his previous endeavours and I know that this seventh hole will soon bring it to the surface in order for him to continue with his training. Only I can see that the reward for his efforts on the sixth will be the painful experience of heartbreak on the seventh. Odd as it may sound to say it; this is not a fault in his game but it is simply the way this course has been designed.

In the meantime he stands on the teeing area mulling over the shot ahead of him and he eventually decides to take a four iron from his bag. His practice swing was loose and carefree as if he had come through the worst of his trials and so his intensity and focus has become momentarily dimmed. The shot when it was played then was naturally a wild one without any control and it sliced horribly away to the right and way out into the deep rough by the side of the green. In amazement I turned my head back towards him and watched as he royally slammed the head of his club down into the ground. Evidently frustrated, he then yanked the bag of clubs around his shoulders and stomped off down the slope. After seeing this powerful and unbridled show of emotion I know that it is best for me to follow carefully at a safe distance behind.

We began to search frantically for his ball and eventually found it in a truly horrid looking spot. It was buried down deep into the long grass, which I knew would be challenging enough in itself to release it from. Not only that; ahead there were those tall trees to think about as they were stubbornly blocking the path between him and the hole at the back of the green. In seeing the difficulty of the shot he has to play he breathes a deep and frustrated sigh and immediately looks to me for guidance.

'Remember what I said to you on the sixth about complete acceptance and non-resistance to your situation. Your ball is here in the deep rough. Don't fight it; don't run away from it; just face it with complete courage of awareness. This may not be where you think you should be on the golf course but this is where you are. Now tell me what happens if you can look at it without any fear and without that mind of judgment.'

He is quiet for a moment as he looks deeply at where his ball lies. In the process I notice how the restless frustration that he was not yet through the worst of his trials was beginning to ease almost as quickly as it had flared. The teaching of the sixth has clearly served him well.

'I feel at peace,' was his direct and simple answer.

'You don't feel humiliated to be here?' I probe further.

'Not in this moment, no.'

'Very good.'

The moment soon passes though as his mind jumps straight back in with a question.

'But how does this peace help me get my ball out of the rough?'

'It helps you a lot more than when you didn't have it,' I reply sharply.

He looks at me puzzled as if wondering what to do next. Should he try and have a swing at it? Should he take a penalty stroke and drop the ball in a more favourable spot? Should he go all the way back to the teeing area and play the shot again? I can see all these thoughts moving through his mind and I know I must give more instruction.

'Remember also what I said about it being solely in your hands how you swing the club. What happens if you try and swing at the ball in this state of peace?'

He pulls out a pitching wedge and takes a dubious look as if wondering how on earth he is going to get the ball out of there with it. He stands there and takes a couple of swings before giving an almighty hack into the deep rough. Tufts of grass have gone flying again but the ball fails to emerge. Instead it has only been buried more deeply...as in truth I had imagined it would be.

He looks up at me heartbroken as if somehow he'd been expecting a miracle to occur from my instruction and that his actions had somehow made it worse.

'Can you accept and be at peace in this moment or do you still think you should be somewhere better than here,' is my only instruction.

'*Well I can't stay here all day can I?*' he answers exasperatedly.

And there it was; in those few words the subtle wound of the seventh revealed itself in all of its glory!

'Do you expect the instruction from the sixth to take you somewhere other than where you are now then?' I immediately ask; latching upon his admission of weakness.

'Well of course I do!' he answers without a moment's

hesitation 'It's not much fun is it spending my time hacking away here in the rough getting nowhere.'

'So deep down you are trying to use the teaching of acceptance and non-resistance as a strategy to successfully get somewhere else...or should I say to avoid something. Deep down your mind is using what you learned on the sixth as a way to stay in control.'

'I don't understand.'

'Look I know well enough how it is ingrained within your psyche that effort must lead to reward; and not only that but the reward must be given instantaneously. Deep within you still believe that success lies outside of you and that it is something that must be obtained. Deep within you still believe that who you are in your essence is nobody and deep within you still believe that you need to get somewhere else in order to be *somebody*. You are quite willing to use these spiritual teachings as much as any other teaching if they lead to this end but if they don't help you get out of the rough then you are quite happy to discard them. Is that about right?'

'But what is wrong with the ambition to do something more with my game than just hack around like a numpty here in the deep rough?'

'There's nothing wrong with ambition and striving. I am just teaching you not to attach *who you are* to the outcome of those strivings. Let me tell you that who you are is as perfect here as it is if you'd have nailed your tee shot onto the green. But if you falsely attach your self esteem and your symbols of power to something external then your strength as a warrior is going to be severely compromised. The true warrior does not need to defeat his opponent in order to prove his worth.'

'I see. But I still don't understand how all of that helps me to play this shot at hand.'

'Just enjoy the journey and stop worrying about the outcome of where it is taking you. Keep on remembering the instruction that you can't control what hand you are given in this moment...but you can control how you choose to play it.'

'So how can I play the hand that has been given to me here?'

'The last hole was about the 'Two H's' of Humility and Humour. This hole is about the 'Three P's' of Patience, Persistence and Perseverance.'

'So you are saying I should just keep taking the shot until the ball comes out then?'

'Not necessarily. When water comes up against solid rock it has to yield and find another way. The teaching of the 'Three P's' does not encourage you to be rigid and dogmatic in your approach but it does give you the stamina to hang in there for the long haul in working your way around and through the many obstacles on the path. Only those who remain attached to the outcome flinch at the first sight of resistance. They are the ones who will fold their hand rather than play it through to the end.'

'Ah, so this hole is to do with the element of water then is it?' he asks, eagerly jumping upon my analogy.

'That's right.'

'Can you please teach a little more about this element?'

'I'd be delighted to. To begin with I want you to imagine for a moment that you are a drop of rain that has fallen upon a mountain summit. Now looking down from here you can see the ocean that is your ultimate destination. Yet watch and see that the drop of water does not plough through the most direct route in order to reach its end. For the drop of water knows that life consists of the journey as much as the ending and it goes forth to meander its way down across the terrain and follows the due course that it is guided to take. It seems in no great hurry to get to the ocean because it has not attached its own power and self esteem to this great body of water. Instead it knows without question that the essence of the ocean is itself held within this single drop. There is no separation between here and there. On its journey it is completely at one and at peace with wherever it finds itself and it just surrenders and allows the force of gravity to move it wherever it needs to be moved to. It doesn't try to control the process in order to get there much quicker. It lives with complete patience and trust that it will be guided wherever it needs to be guided and that it will reach wherever it needs to reach in its own perfect time.

'Now the natural movement of that drop of water gives a teaching that is the total opposite of what you have been taught out there in the world. Out there you have been taught that the ocean is separate from you and that you must get there as quickly and as directly as you can…no matter who or what you trample on in the process. Modern man has absolutely no patience or trust to surrender his control to a force that will meander him slowly across the landscape of his life. If he did he would have to be willing to carry out tasks without the promise of instant success or reward. He may even have to turn his back on his ultimate destination in order to follow the true course in the moment. And do you know why he is so unwilling and in such a rush?'

'No,' he answers bewilderedly.

'It is because he is trying to avoid his feelings and is unable to fully embrace what they contain. You long for your ball to be on the smooth green and it has *sliced* open your heart to find your ball right here. You don't want to feel that pain of heartbreak within and so you skip past that step and dive into the reaction of your emotions. You become anxious, angry, frustrated and you plough ahead insensitively with your game without due care. It is this carelessness that causes the 'Three P's' to be abandoned. Yet it is a paradox that it is only the one who overcomes their fear and dives through the sheer pain of heartbreak who will come through to the other side to realise that the pain is only an illusion.'

'An illusion? How can you say it is only an illusion when that sliced shot cut so deep? I must have felt it otherwise I wouldn't have gotten so angry about it.'

'It becomes an illusion once you realise that though you desire the ball to be on the green; being here does not make you any less that who you already are. As I say; as a drop of water you realise that the ocean is inside of you wherever you are on the course and nothing that happens out here can change your innate perfection. Once again, like all the other fears we have worked through, the fear of heartbreak has its strength when it hides in the darkness. Bring it into the light and you will see it is all smoke and mirrors.'

'So you are saying that I need to hang in there with where I am at this moment in the game and to just stay in touch with my feelings so that they no longer hold their power over me?'

'That's right. It is about being absolutely consistent in the midst of life's many ups and downs. This is what the Lord of Equanimity offers as a way to deal with the many heartbreaks that you will taste during this lifetime. This doesn't mean that you become cold and distant from your game but it simply means that you can dive through it without getting fazed or overwhelmed by it. You can only do this by staying completely present and awake in its midst.'

'So even though this game will always break me; I still have to go through it with eyes wide open?'

'Yes. You have to be willing, but not want, your heart to be broken by the game if you are to carry on playing it. Otherwise, if you are not willing then it will remain a torturous game for you to play and you will be forced to carry on going through this rollercoaster of intense emotions that hold you in their power.'

'But how can this heartbreak be such a good thing to endure?'

'It is truly a grand thing that you care enough about the game to want to hit that ball on the green rather than to slice it out here in the deep rough. But the price of your love and care is the price of heartbreak that has to be paid because eternal salvation can never be found through this game. No matter how hard you try, it cannot lead you to a promised land where nothing painful will touch you ever again.'

'So why must I care then about my game? Why not go through it with a closed heart and to just plough on insensitively?'

'That goes right back to the impossible question you asked on the second as to why you have to play the hand that has been given. You just have to play it as best you can and that's all there is to it. All you need to know is that the heart is made to be broken again and again much like the leaves must fall in the autumn in order for new growth to emerge in the spring. Only the courageous know that nothing can be ultimately lost in this process of heartbreak and renewal. In fact everything is to be gained.'

'So you are saying that those who struggle on hoping for the best are missing the whole point of the game?'

'Yes because their resistance is inevitably futile. They are so brittle that one slice holds the power to turn them away from the game for good. They fall like a house of cards because they have no firm foundations; they have no strong underbelly to stomach the challenges of this game unless they are given a guarantee that it will soon lead them to salvation. They are the ones who need to find a reason why bad things happen; they need to see a purpose in all this suffering created by the way the course and the game has been designed. They are the ones who scratch their heads and think that though they cannot see it; there must surely be some higher plan involved in the creation of all these golfing hazards. Or else; rather than trees, rough and bunkers; why did God not just make the seventh into one big green with a ten-foot diameter hole? Or make that twenty-foot even? Little wonder that they have no patience for the vagaries of this game when no reason is given and little wonder that they throw a tantrum and are swiftly defeated by it.'

'Okay I think I am beginning to get what this seventh is trying to teach. But I still don't understand how I need to go forward and complete this hole. If water comes up against solid rock how does it decide which way to get around it?'

'Look just stop trying to control the process! You need to learn to open up, surrender, and allow divine will to work in and through you. All you have to do is let it show you the best course of action to take by being fully available to it in this moment.'

'I see. And by being fully available you mean being fully present in my heart and its feelings.'

'Yes that's right. Your feelings are the gateway through which you must pass and only those who are willing to be touched by heartbreak will realise it.'

'And my feelings will then guide me from there?'

'Yes but I can't tell you what that looks like. You have to attune and connect with your own intuition and figure it out for yourself. But remember what I say about releasing your attachment to the outcome as it will never work out this way. You can't get an intuitive hunch on how to get to B from A because it is only your mind that tells you that B is the next destination...and in truth this may not be the right destination you need to go to. Intuition is never a prophecy of the future but is always real and practical in the moment. Intuition only serves to give instruction on the next immediate step forward from the here and now.'

'So you are saying that I can't seek guidance on how to get the ball on the green from here?'

'No absolutely not! You can only seek what your next shot needs to be...and then, as I have said before, to play the shot the best you can by honouring your timing.'

He goes quiet as if beginning to attune and connect with what to do next. It is another good sign of progress that he is learning to look within himself for guidance rather than relying on me to lead him by the hand around the course. It is a good sign in this fledgling warrior that he is finally prepared to develop and to draw upon his own inner resources of power to get him through the challenges he is facing. He is no longer so consumed by blind emotion.

'I think I will move the ball and take a penalty shot for it.'

'Very well but you must trust that yielding is a sign of strength and not of weakness. Remember that it is the one who does not follow his own felt intuition who is ultimately the weaker of the two...even if he may appear to be more flamboyantly courageous in the eyes of others. Never confuse the hero's loud grandstand gesture with the warrior's more measured response. You must always remember the importance of the Three P's.'

He is allowed to move the ball two clubs length away from its current buried location and there is a patch of lighter rough that he is able to drop the ball into. He does so and it drops into a spot where it rests more accessible to hit. It will still be a tough fourth shot to play but again he wisely connects in to his feelings and inner source of wisdom in order to get a sense of the right shot to play. The trees are too high to play over and to play a shot under the low lying branches would be a high risk shot. Wisely, I feel, he takes out a wedge with the intention of hitting a shot to the left of the trees where he just has a glimpse of the front fringe to aim for. The question is how closely does he flirt with those branch arms in order to get as close as possible to the hole?

The swift answer is that his aim is slightly wayward and he gets far too close. The ball smacks into wood and drops straight down to the ground. But this small error matters not in the grand scheme of things as I am more concerned now with his response to this new situation. I watch then as he walks forward to where his ball is now lying and I watch approvingly as I see that the anxiety and restlessness has dissipated away and he is no longer in a state of panic that the numbers are piling up on his scorecard. It feels as if the boy who would have once tried to pull off the bold shot of recovery, or blindly hoped for a miracle, is beginning to grow up and to mature for the long haul of the game.

From here in the lighter rough it is more straightforward to play a low running long-iron shot through a gap and he judges this shot well as it rolls to a halt just shy of the flag. Two further strikes of the putter follow before the ball is sunk and he walks off the green and diligently records a quadruple bogey seven upon his scorecard.

The Lord of Commitment

Having grasped the lesson of patience on the seventh hole I feel he is ready to face the fourth test of power and the fourth situation that may cause his golf club to wobble. Once more this hole is perfect for this test because it appears to the naked eye to be thoroughly uninteresting in its design. It is a par-four of 400 yards in length and it pans out in a dead-straight fashion with a wide fairway leading to a green at its end. The rough on either side was light and unassuming and there were no hazards between the tee and the green. Not even one bunker had been carved into the landscape here. One glance tells us both that this hole was created as an afterthought by the ones who had designed the course. Cynically he would probably hazard a guess that this was the last hole that they had planned and that they had run out of their budget and their creative juices to jazz it up with interesting features and challenges. It truly appeared to be a hole of disinterest but for me it served perfectly to mirror his new state of cool detachment from the game.

With nothing around here to inspire or motivate, I watch as his appetite for the game disappears immediately into a sluggish fuzz of ambivalence. His well of zeal has dried up and, as he gives a few limp practice swings, I notice that there is no longer a special zing to his swing. He is standing here on the tee and he is almost going through the motions in his movements. Naturally, in this state, his golf will almost certainly remain a little off key and off rhythm.

So the strike when it comes is neither sweet nor wild and the ball merely bounds along its own merry way. He bends down to pick up the tee peg and I watch astounded as he doesn't even bother to see what has happened to it and where it has ended up. Confusedly he has become content with his wayward striking of the golf ball and he now has no obvious desire to coax this ball into the hole and to improve his scorecard. His newly accepting nature contains a blind spot within it that must now be brought out into the light on the eighth.

So I walk a few steps behind and watch as he ambles along the fairway as if he no longer has a care in the world. Having suffered the cost of becoming too tight over the previous three holes…he is now suffering the cost of having become too loose. He is off the middle path and his club has already begun to wobble once more. And I know all to well that once he slips off this hallowed ground that it will be very challenging for him to find and to get back on it again.

He approaches where the ball lies and he hardly gives a second thought about the shot he wants to play down here. The lack of sweetness from his drive has left him with a long iron shot to play and it will be a struggle to get the ball onto the green from this far back. But he just seems more obsessed about protecting his timing than anything else. As a result; though his swing is smooth and graceful I see none of his power and presence radiating down through the shaft of the golf club like I did back on the fourth hole when he sent the ball flying out of bounds. So again it is a strike that is neither sweet nor wild and it merely lands and bobbles its way down in the vague direction of the desired destination. The time has come for me to intervene.

'What did I teach you back yonder about your relationship with your golf club?' I ask forcefully; taking the club from his hands in the process.

He looks at me with trepidation as if wary of being given another lecture.

'Was it something to do with teaching me about my

relationship with power?' he responds; with a sigh of relief at having retrieved that priceless piece of information from somewhere deep within his memory.

'I am not interested in hearing you repeat back to me the words you can memorise. I want to see you put them into practice. Tell me where your power is in your golf club now?' I snap right back at him.

'I don't know,' he stutters back; possibly unsure in that moment whether any answer could possibly satisfy me.

'That is because it is not there is it? Now tell me where has the zeal to improve your game gone?'

'Wait a minute. Haven't you been the one teaching me these past few holes to stop being so zealous in my approach to the game and to be less obsessed about the outcome?' he protests in abject confusion.

'When will you learn what I tell you about the middle way? Do you remember when I said to you that the teaching is only contradictory because you are contradictory? You have still to learn to go beyond these extreme swings. Just because I taught you to be less attached to the outcome, does not mean that it is okay for you to no longer care about your game.'

'But how on earth can I possibly know that I am off the middle way this time!'

'This way of complete balance is what you must learn in order to be a true warrior in this world. The key is always to be mindful and in the moment and to know instantly when your golf club begins to wobble. And when you do catch it wobbling, which it inevitably will, it is vital that you stop and see what is causing you to fall off balance in order to right yourself instantly. Don't let it drag on for another second for if you do it becomes so much harder to get back on track.'

'But I am being vigilant and I am putting into practice all you've taught me these last few holes! Can't you see how detached, humble and patient I am being here!'

'Do not be so rigid and complacent in propping yourself safely to the middle road on the one side whilst neglecting all the other influences that may be pulling you off on the other side. A true warrior is always well rounded so that he may not be easily toppled. He is the master of all situations that may otherwise cause him to give away his power mindlessly. He is an expert in the art of containment and is not easily defeated.'

'So what influence is pulling me off balance on this hole then?'

'This is the element of earth. It is an element that gives rise to the illusion that life is set in stone; that life is fixed, solid and permanent. It gives the illusion that life is predestined by forces that lie outside of your influence. It can be a suffocating force that leaves one feeling powerless and claustrophobic by its rigidity.

'The element of earth can then lead to the false fatalism that the cards will fall where they fall and a belief that the power to influence and shape that destiny lies outside of your hands. With the equanimity you have gained towards the practice on an emotional level you now no longer feel the desire to make a commitment on the physical level. The levelling of your mood has given way to a powerless shrug of your shoulders in the face of this indomitable foe.'

'But why is my physical commitment so important?'

'Because without this commitment your golf club eventually wobbles that is why! Let me be clear that this is a subtle force at work here that can easily slip through your defences. The last three holes have been easy for you to work with because the challenges have been more prominent in your face. You've really had to raise your game in order to navigate your way through these holes. But this hole gives a different challenge because having raised your game...the work now begins to keep it there.

'For this hole marks the fallow periods in your life where nothing much is engaging the interest of your senses and mind. These are the quiet times in your exterior world and it can be easy to lose your enthusiasm and zest and your sense of purpose. These are the times when you would really rather be doing something else than hitting a golf ball around a field because it is no longer stimulating your appetite as it perhaps once did. In truth these are the most dangerous moments where your golf club can wobble and the Lord of Commitment can come and easily take away your power and poise. Therefore it is absolutely critical in these moments to renew again and again your commitment to the game so that you may keep this particular phantom at bay.'

'Well how do I begin to renew my commitment?'

'To start with you need to recognise where your freedom lies and where the power of personal choice exists. It is especially helpful to remember in these moments what it was that first took you through the gate and onto the golf course. Can you remember back in the beginning how you had the open and curious mind that was fascinated with learning about what this game was all about. Back then you were intrigued by this quirky game and its challenges of bunkers, water hazards and deep rough. You were adventurous and so willing to dive into whatever the game had to offer you. Committing to the game seemed easy way back in the beginning because it was something new and exciting. But now on this eighth hole all this quirkiness has been taken away from you and there is nothing here to stoke your fire and to keep your appetite alive. This is a barren place and the time has come for you to dig deep in your own reserves and to draw upon the well of enthusiasm that lies deep within you. On this eighth hole the game no longer does the leverage for you.'

'I see. But I don't quite understand how remembering what it was like in the past can help me through this hole now.'

'Well a reminder like this will always help you turn your attention back towards the middle way that you have fallen off. It immediately gets you back into your shoes and in your power because you suddenly start to remember again that yes you do want to be here.'

'And once I've reaffirmed my choice to be here then what

then?'

'Well you have to look at ways to spice the game up a little to keep the fire stoked during these bleak moments. For instance you could take a look around you and take time to appreciate the sky and the beauty of these natural surroundings. That is one way to bring you back to a place of appreciation and gratitude for being here in the moment. Another way would be to shake up your swing a little to pull you out of your monotonous routine. Instead of just playing a standard iron shot that you've just struck why not play a little low running shot, or have a little fun by playing a big fade or a draw down this rather boring looking straight hole. And when you are down by the green why don't you play a little bump and run or a high lob onto the green rather than just striking a standard monotonous chip with your wedge. I don't know; just do anything to change things up and to get your interest engaged again in your practice.'

'Well can you remind me again what fear I need to overcome on this hole?'

'This is all to do with the fear of disappointment. There is now a part of you that is willing to go through the motions of performing the script you have been given but deep within you have the suspicion now that it will only serve to ultimately disappoint you. With this suspicion in hand you are refusing to put any more enthusiasm into the game than you really have to.'

'But why do I think it will disappoint me?'

'Well I think that happens because it is not panning out here as you first thought it might. The hero comes out here hoping for the fairytale ending from the game; but as long as you hold on to these hopes and dreams you will also have to hold onto this fear on the other side of the coin. To grow up from an immature hero to a real warrior requires you to abandon this hope altogether.'

'I thought the last hole was about getting rid of my hope of salvation and the fairytale ending?'

'Yes and no. You might have released your demands for a

painless existence within the unfolding story; but you still have hopes that your patience will eventually be rewarded somehow.'

'And what's so wrong with being the hero who dares to dream the impossible dream anyway?' he protests animatedly.

'Your dreams only drain you of your power if you don't take action to make them happen. I want you to remember what I said about the element of earth giving rise to the illusion that life is already set in stone. Well let me say now that the hero, rather than being sidelined by this illusion, actually convinces himself that his life is predestined for something great. He believes that great and unstoppable forces are at work and pushing him on towards greatness. But in truth it doesn't really matter whether this illusion of predestined forces inspires or deflates you; either way you are still giving the game a power over you that it doesn't truly have.'

'So I shouldn't delude myself by dreaming big then?'

'Dreaming big isn't the problem; you will discover this in due course. But look, let me be clear about what I am saying here right now. What I am saying is that the hero is infantile and you must never draw on this archetypal force to try and overcome the Four Lords we have been facing. The Hero, though he appears brave at first glance, is really the child in you who ultimately lacks the discernment, the humility, the patience and the discipline to get through these four tests. And so let me tell you that it is solely because of your heroic daydreams that you have now fallen off the path down here.'

'Really? I didn't know that I was daydreaming down here?'

'Well it didn't start here. Subtly the Achilles heel that is the Hero's Dream has been lurking there ever since the second; but until now you've been able to keep that dark truth hidden beneath the surface because there have been other things going on to mask this most deep rooted of fears. But now on this eighth hole we can see how this deep lying root is causing your golf club to wobble. It is the ripe time now to illuminate this fear in order so that it drains power and vital energy from you no more.'

'Why has it been lurking since the second?'

'On the second you renewed your vow of incarnation and so the Hero's Dream was unleashed. Back then you hoped that, although it was a difficult quest, fulfilling that vow would lead you to a promised land. It is here on this eighth hole, however, that this promised land is nowhere to be seen. It has vanished.'

'Well if that's the case, I don't see how changing up my swing or looking up at the sky will help overcome these hopes and fears. Isn't that all a bit superficial?'

'You're right; but don't confuse the means for the ends. The key way to overcome your fear of disappointment is by renewing your vows for being here and to recognise that this is indeed what you have chosen. You have to keep telling yourself that no matter how the script pans out, that there is nowhere else you would rather be than here in these shoes. I was just suggesting that changing up your swing may be one way to help you renew this vow and to keep it fresh. It may help keep you in the moment when there is nothing else that is pulling you there.'

'But wait a minute here. You were the one who told me back on the second that I don't have a choice but to play this part?'

'Yes I said that you don't have any choice over being here; but you do have choice over *how* you be here. How do you choose to handle the script in your hand? Do you choose to see it as an impossible burden that has been placed on your shoulders or a generous gift? Do you see it as a punishment? Or do you see it as a blessing?'

'So you are saying it is wiser to see the script as something I've chosen rather than something that has been imposed?'

'Not only that but you also see it as something chosen without those rose-tinted spectacles on. You don't delude yourself with any false illusions about where the story might be heading. You accept it all with eyes wide open.'

'I see. And by doing this I will no longer fear being disappointed by it? It will no longer have that power over me?'

'That's right. This is the only way that you can get through this eighth hole. For if you see it as imposed against your will, or if you falsely believe it to be something it is not, then I don't see how you can truly stand in your power when playing the story out. If these were your beliefs, I don't see how you can stop your club from wobbling as it has already down here. Hope may have got you through the last three holes but hope has now become your downfall.'

'I see. And so you are also saying that I won't be trusted with anything significant on the holes to come unless I affirm that this is what I choose with my eyes wide open,' he answers as the penny drops and he finally appreciates what this hole is about.

'That's correct,' I reply with a nod. 'The element of earth teaches that *your commitments must always be founded on truth not illusion*,' I add as I point him directly towards the core instruction of this hole. 'Otherwise if they are not then you will be found wanting when that illusion is exposed; as it eventually will.'

We walk on in silence as he begins to absorb the teaching of the eighth in his heart. I watch as his head turns skywards as he tries to find the generosity of spirit in order to feel grateful to be having this experience here now. The fear of disappointment has been illuminated and has nowhere left to hide. His spirit begins to soar as we saunter more purposefully down this eighth fairway towards the spot where his ball has come to rest in the light rough.

There are only fifty yards or so left between him and the flag and he takes on my advice by pulling out a lob wedge from the bag. There is plenty of room beneath the ball to get it up high and to give it some air. He takes a few full practice swings of the club as he tries to judge how much loft and how much power to give the shot. His imagination has been captivated and the spark is alive in his eyes as he finally makes his approach before the ball. The shot is ultimately well judged and the ball glides gracefully down onto the green with a soft landing and without much roll. He turns to me with a wide smile that showed his passion for the game had truly been rekindled. From here two further putts of the ball followed before it sank into the cup and another bogey five was safely recorded upon the scorecard.

Placing the flag back in the cup I breathe a sigh of relief that the four Lords have all now been faced. Though not ultimately conquered, he at least knows where they hide and how to illuminate the fears that give them their power. He knows enough to move on to the ninth and the final hole of this front half of the course.

The Keys of Manifestation

We leave behind the eighth green and there is an enthusiastic bound to his step that is most welcome to see. He is walking with a keen sense of earnest towards the ninth hole and with a newly restored appetite for what it may bring. This is the hole that is ranked as the most difficult on the course; covering the longest yardage of all of the ten par fours as it stretches out nearly 460 yards before us. It is a hole that slopes steeply uphill and it dog-legs slightly to the left with numerous pothole bunkers carved into the fairway to serve as a test of accuracy and luck. The green is large and the most undulating one on the course as it spanned out with many rolling hills and valleys. I knew that this was the one green on the course that would really reveal how well he is attuned to the feel of his game.

Before taking the club from his bag he looks across at me for instruction almost as if asking what was to come next now that he had navigated his way through the four tests. I give a warm smile in return.

'Yes it is true that you have learned a little now of how to hold your golf club well in this world and to gain some insights into the four fears that cause it to wobble. You will have to come back and play these holes many times to practice and practice again what you have been taught; but for now it is safe for us to continue on with the game. Let me say to you here that to succeed at this ninth hole you must not only know how to hold your golf club wisely; but you must be willing to now use it and to bring it to bear on your game. It is time for you to go forth and to fulfil your creative human potential.'

His eyes widen at the powerful invitation I was laying down before him. It was an invitation to go forth and to maximise his earthly fortune with the golf club that was in his hands. It was so tempting in fact that all the trials he has come through to get to this place of unbounded opportunity are swiftly forgotten.

'Am I really ready to take such a step!' he exclaims with as much excitement as fear in his voice by the prospect.

'Yes and I will now teach you the keys of manifestation,' I reply taking the driver from the golf bag and passing it to him. 'To begin; the first step requires you to visualise a memory of a sweetly struck shot you've struck before. Not the memory in the mind, where we have already learned that it only poisons you, but the memory of a feeling in your heart.'

'What is the difference between the two,' he interrupts.

'The memory of the heart brings you more fully to the present whereas the memory of the mind keeps you in the past,' I reply simply. 'Now I want you to connect with that warm and positive feeling as you approach the shot and to use it as your doorway through. Then see how that feeling influences the shot you play.'

'A doorway?' he asks in puzzlement.

'Yes. Do you remember me saying back yonder that the heavenly hosts are right behind your decision to be here on this course? Well they have in their hands a tremendous power that they are waiting for you to take from them. They want you to succeed and to be all that you can possibly be in this world…and not just to be someone who spends all his time and energy merely finding and holding his balance. Now this doorway is there to help connect you to that power source.'

'But isn't this all just another Hero's Dream? Am I not setting myself up for more disappointment by thinking that this is my destiny?'

'A very wise point indeed,' I respond approvingly. 'But now is the time to see that the subtle difference between the Hero's and the Warrior's Dream is the same subtle difference between an attitude of expectation and an attitude of expectancy. One is your Achilles heel; and the other has the power to propel you to greatness.'

'I think that's far too subtle for me to grasp,' he answers scratching his head uncertainly.

'What I am saying is that over these last few holes we have been busy dismantling all of your childish expectations that are based on a sense of personal entitlement. But this wasn't done to belittle you completely into the dust but to help reveal where your source of true power lies. It seems hard to grasp but in this universe you are both vitally significant and yet utterly insignificant at one and the same time.'

'So you are saying that an attitude of expectancy will help me navigate through this absurd paradox?'

'Yes; most definitely. You open your arms to the miracle of creation that has its power working in and through you; but at the same time you make sure that you don't get caught up in the illusion of entitlement. You don't get caught trying to possess and direct that power for your own ends.'

'And if I am not feeling expectant then you are saying that this power won't come to me.'

'That's right. You have to make the contact otherwise you will simply remain in this stunted adolescent stage of development.'

'But a lot of people I know seem to have grown up just fine and I don't think they believe in these heavenly hosts, or have an expectant mindset that their life is destined for great things.'

'Your kind are well trained in giving the impression that they are living the good life; but if you scratch beneath the surface I think you will see in all a deep rooted fear and emptiness. Many are coping; but I would say it is rare to find someone who is truly thriving in their God given power.'

'And why do you think it is such a rare thing?'

'Do you not remember how hard it was for you to leave your tribe and to step through onto the golf course? You must understand that the whole scheme of your world has been set up to breed conformity with scant regard for the genius that lies within each living person and that is waiting to be unleashed. The tribe fears that its future health will be destroyed if individual's are encouraged to go forth and fulfil their soul's destiny because they know that to do so that they would end up breaking free of their common past and of a tradition that they themselves hold dear. That is why there is tremendous pressure on your shoulders to doubt your own inner wisdom and truth. Realise then that your peers are far more comfortable with you as a low grade hacker like them than as a confident golfer who goes forth to tame this course by your steady hand. Doubt is a force that is ingrained deep within your psyche in order to keep your power contained so that it may be controlled. And if someone should dare to step boldly forth, and to speak of dreams they wish to manifest, they will have to risk being ostracised and distrusted by those around them. He will be a figure that is treated with envy, jealousy and a whole range of other emotions. It is an interesting thought to ponder that there are few in history who have ever achieved genuine greatness in any field and who have received society's encouragement and approval except as an afterthought. Anyone who has dared to fly higher than everyone else has always had to go and do it the hard way as an outsider.'

'You make my world all sound terribly depressing,' he answers ruefully.

'That may be so but this is the scheme on the earth that you have to navigate your way through. It is a scheme designed to test your resolve and the one who finds the way to break free of these constraints is the one who will have truly earned that right. To resist the chorus of naysayers and to hold firm to the vision you wish to create is the real key to success on this hole.'

'But I still don't really understand why these doubters exist? To be honest I am still struggling to accept that my friends and family don't want the best for me.'

'They want the best for you but can only give you that from the knowledge they have of what is best for them. They cannot picture you being a successful golfer when they themselves are still hacking around in the rough. You are asking for a perfect unconditional love from an imperfect race. It is impossible!'

He falls silent again as if still grieving his absence from the familiar. Those vines of guilt haven't yet been cut away from his ankles completely.

'Do you want to go back to being a low grade hacker who preserves the status quo and the world order that is already known and familiar? Or do you still want to take that step into the unknown?'

'It remains a tough dilemma,' he admits honestly.

'That is why such an act is confined to the legends of mythic tales; stories that apparently have no relevance in the real world.'

'What about the Mandela's, the Gandhi's, the Mother Teresa's of this world. Did they not dare to dream the impossible dream?'

'They did but they still had to go through tremendous hardship over long periods of time and to pursue their dreams as outsiders before the world finally came around to recognising their genius. Their stories are inspiring but they hardly set out an easy roadmap for the rest of society to follow.'

'And what about all those sporting heroes around the world? Or those who pursue artistic dreams? Do they not count?'

'They do, but at the same time these are groups of people who have been herded into an arena where mere mortals cannot go unless they have this mysterious thing called talent to get them through the gate. These geniuses become inaccessible to the rest of the world and sadly they often suffer terribly because they are placed in an isolated bubble of precociousness. Sportsmen and artists, because of the way the scheme has been setup, often have deeply troubled and complex private lives as they struggle to integrate their talent in one field across the whole of their life. Again they hardly set out an easy roadmap for the rest of society to follow.'

'But despite all of these obstacles; you think that living expectantly is still actually a wise thing?'

'Yes never let the naysayers dissuade you with all the road-blocks they have put in place. The only thing is that you must dream for the love of dreaming now and not for the hope that it will take you somewhere better than where you are. Hold out for the miraculous in your life and never play it safe out of fear of the unknown. The road may be long and hard but you must grasp the nettle and seize the potential of each moment of your life. Go forth and live it to the fullest.'

'Are you really sure that this is what I am meant to do?' he asks, his voice wavering.

'Take a look at the natural world for inspiration. Look at the butterfly emerging from the chrysalis, the chick taking its first flight, the flower emerging from the bud. It is only man who speaks fearfully and who holds back in doubt when it comes to fulfilling his destiny. You are alive. It is now time for you to live.'

He falls silent again in awe and I watch as he tries to absorb the tantalising invitation that has been given.

'So let me get clear on this first key of manifestation. You are saying that this doorway leads me through to a source of inner wisdom and power as given to me to be used but not to be possessed.'

'That's correct.'

'And you are saying that all those who I grew up with and who taught me all they knew encouraged me to keep that doorway closed because they never had the courage to enter it themselves.'

'Also correct.'

'And then you are saying that rather than relying on their wisdom that I must resist these doubters and plough through that doorway in order to go further in my game than where I have come to now.'

'Yes. If you don't go through it you will spend the rest of your game merely trying to keep your balance so that the situation in the world doesn't become worse by your actions. That will be as far as you can go.'

'That does sound a bit of a bum deal doesn't it? I mean, I knew when I first came out here that I was ruffling some feathers with my odd behaviour; but this just seems to take it to a whole new level. Then I was just curious and now it all seems a bit more serious. I can't help wondering whether this whole adventure isn't all a bit narcissistic.'

'That depends on where you take these keys of manifestation and how well you handle these new powers. Like Icarus; those who fly too close to the sun are always at risk of getting their wings burnt. But if you only intend to use this power for good in the world then surely it is wise to not cut off your power source with doubts and fear. Let me say again that you serve no-one by staying in the tribal role assigned to you and by doing your duty. Believe me when I say that the world desperately needs your genius to shine forth.'

He accepts what I say with a gentle nod of understanding and I begin to observe as he puts my first instruction into practice whilst taking a few practice swings of the club.

'Very good,' I say as I watch his energy field become clearer and lighter as the warm feeling takes root in his awareness.

At the sound of my words he steps forward and plays the shot; and he indeed strikes it straight and true towards the target. Amazingly he has managed to stumble upon the doorway instantly and I watch and see how enthused he has become with the teaching of the first key. He too has felt the subtle difference.

'What you are saying is all quite new from what you've taught me until now…but I have to say it all sounds very exciting,' he adds before we walk on together in silence.

I watch approvingly and see how he has remained devoted to the practice we learned on the fourth of not giving away this precious gift before his next breath comes. His mindfulness is running true now and it is pleasing to see that this fledgling warrior is starting to build steel in his boots.

We come to a halt where the ball lies, but before he takes the second shot I need to expand on the instruction I gave back on the teeing area.

'Once you have found and entered the doorway, the next key of manifestation is to dispel all other remaining doubts. You have overcome the doubts of your tribe but now you have to overcome the doubts that lie within your own mind and to leave them at the door too. For with a mind of doubt it is probable that even though your hold of the club will be strong it will not translate through into action. Doubt is a force that inhibits the warrior from standing fully in the power that he has in his hands. To dispel these doubts you must gain confidence that you *can* truly manifest whatever it is the universe yearns to create through your game and through this shot.'

'How can I do this?' he asks curiously.

'You must go in and replace all fearful and negative images with positive ones. To do this you must visualise clearly the shot you now wish to play and then know that it can become realised. Visualise every facet of that shot in your mind's eye; from the flight of the ball to the exact spot of its landing.'

'But hang on a minute,' he reacts instantly. 'You said before on the sixth and seventh that the only thing in my power is the movement of my swing…and that after that the ball will go wherever it is meant to go.'

'That was the instruction when you were learning to handle your power wisely. Now that you can safely walk it is okay to try and run. But to have taught you to run before you could even walk would have been a disaster,' I reply with a wry smile on my face. 'The time is ripe now for you to realise the simple but profound truth that whatever you want to manifest in this world you have to think it first.'

'So I can control where the ball goes with my mind as much

as through my swing then?' he asks in amazement.

'Not as much but wholly. If your thoughts are full of fearful and negative images then no matter how perfect your swing that little white ball will go astray. Do you remember at all what we spoke of on the third hole that it is consciousness that creates matter and that you had to be very vigilant as to what was running through that head of yours?'

'Vaguely,' he answers. He has learned so much since then that the third does seem quite a long time ago in his memory.

'Well now you are ready to go further and flourish according to this law. You must take the responsibility of keeping your thoughts confident and clear because no matter how ropy your swing appears to the naked eye it won't stop you from striking the ball true. That is why there are professional players out there who manage to get away with throwing out the textbook and using the most unorthodox and quirky swings imaginable. This is the sacred law of creation.'

'So you are saying that if I can just remove all negativity and doubt from my mind that I don't have to bother again with all the things I've learned over these past few holes to keep my swing from wobbling?'

'No I am not saying that at all. The soul whose relationship to power is susceptible and shaky will not be able to manifest his potential consistently no matter how confident and clear his mind may appear to be. It goes back to what you learned on the fourth hole that you can't rely on pulling yourself together in the critical moments of the game and to get away with lapses elsewhere. Your devotion must be total and whole and you must trust that every hole on this course has its place in that whole. This isn't an either/or black/white situation. All I am asking here is that you simply honour what is going on in your mind as much as you've been honouring your swing.'

'I didn't really consider it on the third; but it is quite fascinating that I would even have these negative images cropping up in my mind. I mean, if I manifest whatever I am thinking then why is it not natural for me to just focus on thinking positive thoughts?'

'You didn't consider it before because on the third we were simply focused on the effect not the cause of these negative thoughts that pass through your screen. Your lesson then was to learn how to breathe your swing and to gain detachment from them. But the time has clearly come to go deeper into this.'

'So what is causing them then?'

'It is all because of your karma.'

'My karma?'

'Yes, believe it or not you are not here starting from a blank canvas and choosing what it is you want to create upon it from scratch. If that was the case then of course you would choose the positive over the negative. But you would not believe how much mental baggage you have accumulated on that canvas; indeed the whole of human history is written upon it and that history continues to carry an energy charge that perpetuates itself in the present and shapes what happens right now. There are literally a billion thoughts clamouring in your mind at the moment and all of them are trying to have their say about this shot that is at hand. And of course this inherited legacy, this karma of yours, is largely fuelled with unresolved negativity that just lingers on rather than the more positive images which in truth leave no trace in the mind. Look into your memory of the game you have played already and tell me what first comes to mind?'

'The sliced tee shot on the seventh,' he answers honestly after barely a moment's pause.

'Not your tee shot you've just played here? Not your magical wedge on the first?'

'No they didn't come first to mind,' he admits uncomfortably.

'So you see then that we always tend to remember and hold on to the bad shots of our game rather than the great ones. The deep rough is the past of human history and it is a reflex action for you to be drawn there time and again without ever really knowing why. But you are really being drawn their because that is where most of your attention goes. This is the nature of mind and all of this is what you are up against if you truly want to master the keys of manifestation.'

'I still can't believe that my tee shot here on the ninth didn't come to mind first,' he exclaims, demanding a better explanation. 'It was so beautiful and so recent and fresh. Why did I go all the way back to the seventh?'

'Because that tee shot and the magical wedge were taken in the present moment; the one place where mind could not grab it. Remember that your mind only lives for past and future and unchecked it will always take you back into your emotions from what has gone before or into your hopes of what is to come. Your mind will always try and keep you on the same repetitive loop.'

'I see,' he answers reflectively. 'So I have to clear out the mind otherwise I will just keep on manifesting more of the same based on what has gone before. You are saying that in order to manifest my pure potential here and now I have to make a clean break with *everything* that has happened in the past.'

'Exactly. The breathing exercises on the third helped you on this but now you have a bigger purpose for doing so. You are not doing it just for inner peace but to create room for something new and revolutionary to emerge. But remember that this is not meant to be a deep exercise of psychoanalysis. You don't have to go in and weed out every little negative thought that exists in your system for you will do that for an eternity and not even scratch the surface. This is because there are not only your thoughts, but your parent's thoughts, and their parent's thoughts, and so on. And then there are thoughts you have accumulated because of your gender or the country you were born. As I say the whole of human history is literally written within your psyche, and though it is hard to comprehend, there is nothing that has gone before that doesn't influence your way of thinking now. This is because what is in the one is also in the whole.'

'Wow it's mind boggling that there is all that stuff stored away in here. So if I don't have to weed it all out, then how do I free myself from this karma?'

'The only way is to be completely aware of what is arising in the moment and through the practice of illumination to weed out whatever is up *right now.* You don't have to go digging for it. There is always something arising.'

'So it's just like you showed me on the third,' he repeats again.

'Yes. As an example you may notice as you stand here that your mind has an image of you just skewing the ball wildly to the left. The source and reason of that image cropping up is irrelevant because all you have to do is to spot it and to make sure you don't hook yourself upon it. But now you must go even further than we did on the third by bringing in the positive image of the shot you want to play and allow that to take root. By doing this you may begin to manifest something completely new and original than what has gone before. This is where the real revolution takes place in resolving the karmic issues that you are here to deal with. *So go on and tell me what your best vision is for the shot ahead?'*

He looks across at the yardage marker on the edge of the fairway and sees that he still has more than 200 yards to go to reach the green. He then looks down at his lie and sees that the ball is sitting on a hard and dry piece of ground. He then finally looks ahead towards his target and mulls over my question.

'Does my vision have to be realistic?' he asks. 'Because looking at this lie I wouldn't want to take a fairway wood and I know it is impossible for a three iron to get me onto the putting surface. Or by saying that it is impossible am I just hindering what is possible to be achieved here?'

'Trust me; these facts are not doubts you are sharing,' I answer approvingly. 'Manifestation isn't white magic and it isn't a conjuring act where you just pull the rabbit out of the hat from nowhere. Manifestation is simply a transfer of energy from a state of potentiality to a state of existence...and it is impossible to get more out from what you put in.'

'So I can't just stand here and create something out of nothing then?'

'Absolutely not! You can't stand here and manifest your ball onto the green by closing your eyes and just wishing for it! You are a co-creator here in the process and not a bystander. You have to bring forth the energy by swinging your club. This is exactly why everything you have learned so far has been so important because it has served to maximise the amount of creative energy you can bring to the table; and therefore maximises what can be manifested from this shot. That is why you haven't been ready for this lesson before. Being off balance, in fear of tribal rejection, or being drained by karmic thoughts from the past all diminish or destroy the potential of what can be manifested *right now.*'

'But on the fourth hole I managed to hit a five iron a good twenty yards further than I would have thought possible?'

'That was only because you were increasing the amount of creative energy in the shot from what you had learned over the previous three holes. But there are still natural limits as to how far you can hit a five iron…at least on the surface of this earth.'

'Okay, so based on what I feel is possible to achieve, I can picture a spot between those two bunkers up there where I want this three iron to land,' he speaks confidently; pointing out to me the two bunkers that were sitting about 30 yards shy of the green.

'Very good,' I answer as I step back to let him play the shot. 'Always remember to start with the doorway and then let the vision take hold from there. Let no other image distract you from it.'

He takes a couple of practice swings before approaching the ball and I watch as everything begins to get aligned behind his vision for the shot ahead. I can see a tremendous power being unleashed down the shaft of the club and the ball is sent true towards its chosen destination. It was a perfect example of manifestation as the vision became an immediate reality before his eyes. I turn my eyes back towards his and see how blown away he is by these keys of manifestation that I have given. Out in the world he had never made much of a success out of anything as he had always been standing in shoes that were not his to fill. But now his creative juices were flowing and life was lending a very supporting hand. With newfound confidence his spirit was soaring and his game was being taken to heights that he could only have once dreamed of.

He strides forth with the keys of manifestation now lodged safely in his heart and he is already plotting the vision for his third shot. It only requires a simple wedge but I know the run of the green is going to be very difficult to judge successfully. And so it turned out. For although the ball landed almost precisely where he intended it to; it just caught the wrong side of the slope and eventually finished up a good thirty feet from the hole. But I can see there are no signs of wavering doubt in his mind about the poor outcome of his shot and he strides on with a very focused and confident intent. He is not going to let this beautifully carved green get the better of him that easily and his eyes remained firmly pinned on the hole that is his desired destination. It is incredible to see how swiftly he has latched upon the teaching of this ninth hole and has become utterly captivated by this game of manifestation he is now ardently playing. He is beginning to display a bullish competitive streak that has not been on show before now. The risk of becoming consumed by the power he has accessed is beginning to run sky high, and like Icarus, he may already be flying too close to the sun.

But he obviously hasn't risen too high yet; and in this belligerent state it was not really a surprise to me that he was able to conquer this wildly sloping green with its deep valleys and high mountain peaks. A positive and confident mindset can indeed move mountains and so he stood over that putt with only eyes on the hole and he managed to nail that long and treacherous putt for a truly tremendous par.

He clenched his fist and pumped it up and down in the air as the ball dropped gently into the cup. A hollering cry emerged from his mouth as he savoured the fruition of all his training on this hardest of holes; a hole that had just been tamed by his guiding hand. Nonchalantly he turned and walked over to me with the words that I knew would have to come but which I had long been dreading to hear.

'*Thanks for all your help*,' he said flinging his arm out with the   intent of shaking my hand.

The Professional Shop

'**G**o speak to the course professional in the shop,' I answer coldly as I refuse to take his outstretched hand. 'I will wait here for your return.'

He looks at me bemused as if not knowing what he has done wrong; if anything.

'What do you want me to say to him?' he stutters back as he displays the first wavering signs in his confident manner.

'You will know when you get there,' I answer back before waving him away and walking on alone towards the bench that was placed behind the tenth tee. Chagrined by my words, he eventually turned in a daze and walked back down the path to the professional shop

Whilst I was not privy to their conversation I later read these journal notes of what took place in my absence:

After leaving my guide I suddenly felt very alone as I walked down the path towards the clubhouse and the shop next door. I didn't want to go and I didn't understand why my guide had been so insistent that I must. For after sinking that glorious putt across the undulating ninth green there was surely nothing left for me to learn out here. Was he not yet ready for me to buy him that drink in the bar I had promised him and where we could toast my success? But alas it is not yet to be and even though I do not know what I am supposed to speak of; I cannot help but obey his instruction. He has done so much for my game.

The door to the shop was open and I walked in quietly

without noise. The course professional was bent over some papers on his desk and was busy scribbling away so I distracted myself by wandering around the shop and looking at all he had on sale here. He did indeed house an impressive collection of the latest golfing equipment which left me amazed at how far technology had come. I could understand though why my guide had insisted that these were designed to merely cover up the cracks in my mind and would stop me from doing the real work. I just don't see how a fancy putter would have taken away the load from my mind in order to nail that putt on the ninth green. I gathered myself and approached the counter where he finally looked up and noticed my presence.

'Oh hello, I didn't hear you come in. Can I help you?' he asked politely.

'Can I just buy this please,' I answered hurriedly picking up the first object on the desk that I laid my eyes upon. I have to admit that I was feeling a little foolish for being here.

'Have you just completed your game? How did you get on?' he asked as he punched numbers into the till.

'Good,' I replied. 'I've just sunk the most incredible thirty foot putt on the ninth for par which has really put the icing on my game. I'll admit that after parring the first it'd been a long struggle of seven holes without anything better than a bogey to show for it but I finally got in the groove at the end. You should have seen the line I had to try and find across that treacherous green! Up and down and then right to left. But I judged it perfectly and in she went!'

'A par indeed. Well you are blessed as not so many are as lucky or as skilled as you to score a par on the ninth. Do you know that's my favourite hole of them all?' he asks as he shows signs of sharing my enthusiasm for the game.

'Why's that?' I ask curiously.

'Well you'll know yourself that it's the trickiest hole of them all and it really tells me honestly how it is I am playing. I'll level

with you. Even if I am playing off key I can easily bluff my way around the first eight holes and scramble together a good score. But I can't get away with bluffing on the ninth. That hole and that green really serves to test my metal every time and I know I wouldn't be the player I am today without it. I think it is a hole that really sorts out the men from the boys.'

'I know what you mean,' I answer concurringly as I think back to what I have just come through. I knew too that without my guide's instruction up the ninth that I would still be playing the boyish hero who was not quite fulfilling his potential with the game. At last I had found a kindred spirit who seemed to understand where I was at in my game. This conversation was fast becoming more interesting than I could have hoped for.

'Take a look at that picture behind you?' he says pointing to a big framed picture on the far wall. 'Do you know who that is standing over that putt in the image?'

'Of course,' I answer. 'That's Tiger Woods.'

'But do you know that he would not be the golfing legend that he is without the ninth hole? He is my idol because he is by far the greatest ninth hole golfer the game has ever seen! He is the one who sets the standard we all must aspire for.'

'Why do you say that?' I ask with interest.

'Come on have you never watched him in action! My goodness he was the most ruthless golfing warrior that ever set foot on the course. He played with no fear of the game and without a care as to how his competitors were playing. His focus was Zen like and unshakeable and he pursued success relentlessly like a great hunter chasing its prey. No wonder his rivals quaked when they saw that Tiger was on the prowl for he showed no mercy for their weaknesses. Not many have the power to throw a player off his own game but Tiger did just by the mere presence of his name creeping up the scoreboard. No wonder that he is close to becoming the most decorated player in the golfing hall of fame. He inspires me like no other to be the best that I can be at this game. If I were you I would *keep him in mind if you want those pars on the ninth to be more than just a lucky break in your game. He was the perfect model of consistency.'*

Hearing him waxing lyrical about his idol like this leaves me inspired but there was something nagging at the back of my mind as he spoke. It was something my guide had spoken of on the tee of sporting idols who suffered from delusions of grandeur because of their talent and who struggled to integrate their genius away from the sporting arena and into the whole of their lives. It left me feeling a little sad that though this tiger had once been free to prowl and to tear up the course record; he had in truth been caged by society into this bubble of talented precociousness that my guide had said about.

'You speak a lot of him in the past tense. Is that because of the scandals in his private life that rocked him when they broke a few years back?'

'We will not speak of those matters here. Jealousy; that's all this was about. People just don't like those who have a special talent and they will do anything to bring them down to the ordinary. Sadly they got the better of him and he hasn't been the same since.'

As he spoke I began to appreciate the sheer futility of trying to blame my circumstances when I've hit a stray ball. I sometimes succumb and do it, but I just couldn't agree that this would have been enough of a reason for this Tiger to fall on his own sword. His mind was surely too strong and focused to be penetrated by negative opinion; he simply can't have regressed back to a time when his club wobbled out of fear. The fall from grace surely had to be a part then of his inner soul's continuing journey towards wholeness. In that moment it became clear to me that the ninth hole can't mark the game's end but that it must surely be another stepping stone on the way.

'I don't know about that. I thought he just shot himself in the foot by believing himself to be the impeachable genius that people like you said he was...and that he is now back on the long path of redemption. He may not carry the same presence on the course

anymore but he just seems a lot more human now than before. I don't know; he seems more humble, warm and real now than the cold heartless scoring machine who seemed in complete control of his destiny before. He seems more approachable somehow.'

'It's only because he has been brought back down to our own God-forsaken level! How can he be inspirational anymore when his scorecard is just littered with schoolboy errors? How can he set the same standard of what it means to be a success when he has just become more human and weak?'

'There's more to success than a par on the ninth though isn't there?' I find the words just tumbling out. To me these words were once akin to blasphemy and the shocked reaction of the course professional reminded me that it was not always safe to speak these things aloud with strangers.

'You've been spending too long in the company of that man you were with before by the sounds of it. I'd watch out if I were you because if you are not careful he will be pulling you out onto the back nine where only wrack and ruin will follow.'

'What's wrong with playing the back nine?'

'What's wrong is that I hear of people getting lost out there. I am sure that's even what happened to Tiger Woods who was probably bundled roughly off the ninth and then dumped out there somewhere. I just hope he finds his way back and remembers the virtue of what it means to be a successful front nine golfer. I just hope he can get back into his prime.'

'But you haven't got lost out there on the back nine?'

'That's because I've never played it! I know my limits and you would be wise to know your limits too. The back nine's a dangerous and wild place to go and play. That's all I know and that's why I won't touch it.'

'But you are the course professional here! Aren't you meant to know your way around the whole course?'

'My job is to help people fulfil their talents and to teach them how to be as successful at the game as they can be. Keep practicing *and keep building up your consistency with your scoring is my advice. Beyond that is none of my business.'*

'I bet you don't teach others to play the game successfully like my guide did.' I snipe back as I found myself becoming increasingly exasperated with this man's fearful attitude. His fears made me wonder why I had thought the ninth marked the game's end. I wondered perhaps whether it is only because it had brought me back around to the clubhouse where I had begun and had given a false sense of completion. Or had I just gotten intoxicated by the lingering sweet aroma of that perfectly struck putt.

'That man doesn't have a clue as to the rules of the game,' he reacts sullenly. 'I am sure if I looked at your swing that I could iron it out better than he has. And what clubs have you been playing with out there? Kid's toys; that's what they are. Take a look and have a play with some of these clubs and you will see what it means to be a man out there. I guarantee you will be able to hit the ball further and straighter with one of these.'

As our conversation was fast deteriorating I could begin to see why my guide had sent me to speak to him. I could see through this man before me that there was something that I was still missing; something that was not yet fully integrated and made whole within me. I now had the keys of manifestation to be the most decorated golfer like Tiger Woods...and yet realising my earthly potential like that all just seemed empty and hollow. I certainly did not want to spend my life worshipping the image of the perfect golfing warrior like this man did. There had to be pieces in the puzzle that still had to be placed; there had to be more that made up a man than this. It was time to return.

'I think I'll take my chances with the guide I have,' I respond bringing the conversation to a close. 'And you know what. I think if Tiger Woods completes his long journey of redemption through the back nine that he will return and eventually become the greatest golfing champion of the game. He won't achieve it now by taking a step back into the past because, contrary to what you may believe, I now understand that the ninth hole player is a boy who is still

pretending to be a real man.'

With that I bid the course professional a good day and left him to make whatever he wanted to make of my last remark.

The Wisdom of No Escape

He has returned from the club shop to where I am sat wait- ing on the tenth tee and I can see that he holds a look of sadness in his eyes. Barely a moment ago, he had all the confidence in the world after sinking that incredible putt for par…and now the glory had simply vanished into thin air.

'What's become of that hubris of yours?' I prod of him gently with a warm smile of welcome at having seen him return.

'Please forgive me for my arrogance. I know now that I am no longer satisfied to be an expert at this game. I need you to teach me how to be a master,' he responds quietly and solemnly with a bowed head. Without daring to look up he holds out the bag of clubs for me to take from his hands.

I nod my head in recognition of his gesture. To come back out to play the second half of the course is the most difficult and humbling act that he will have to make in the game and I under-stand deeply how much his ego is hurting right now. This is far more humiliating an experience than the one he endured back on the sixth hole for now in returning to the course this has become a humiliation of his own choosing. He is openly admitting that he still has so much left to learn. For the one who showed such skill and expertise on the ninth this is truly a hard truth to swallow.

'In order to become a master on this back nine you will have to let go of everything to which you still cling for let me tell you now that I shall come to take it all. Know now then that this is going to be far more of a step for you to take than the simple one you took to get onto the course in the first place. To pierce the heart of this mystery and to realise the ultimate truth that lies within this game we are playing you will have to confront your deepest fears and to confront all the ways that you desire to escape or hide from that truth; such is its power. So tough is this back nine that there are few who have dared to tackle it…although it is destined for all to come through this gate eventually and to finally realise the ultimate truth. The question is whether your time has come or not. Are you really ready to go deeper into the mystery?'

He looks at me stunned and a little wary of what I am asking of him.

'But that first step onto the course was so hard for me to take. How on earth can this one be even harder!' he exclaims in astonishment.

'Although it may appear to you that I was the one leading you through that front nine; in truth we were still playing the game well within your comfort zone and, believe it or not, it was all being done on your terms. Everything that happened to you on the front nine may have been challenging at times; but to your mind the teaching was at least reasonable and not seen as pure folly for it all had the promise of leading you somewhere better than what could have happened if you'd stayed put on the other side of the gate. Reward would follow risk and there was to be no gain without pain…or so your mind would have you believe. The ninth was the mind's reward for its struggles…and yet you know now how empty and shallow this scheme of self improvement really is.

'So by your own meek admission you have told me that you no longer want to play on your terms and, therefore, as we move down this half of the course you will have to do so on terms that will no longer seem reasonable to your mind. I will ask you again whether you are truly ready for that?'

He hears my words but doubtless he is yet able to grasp them. To him it probably still sounds as if I am going to lead him on a marvellous adventure through this back nine and little does he know what he will be letting himself in for if he agrees.

'Yes I am ready,' he gives his answer firmly with earnest eyes and a keen heart.

'You say you are ready but I promise you now that there will come a time out here when you will betray me and your calling. There will be a time when you will just want to pack it all in.'

'How can you possibly say such a thing! After all that I've just realised master I can assure you that I will never now betray you. There is nothing more I long for now than to complete the course!'

'We shall see, we shall see,' I answer mysteriously; taking the bag of clubs from his outstretched hand and directing him onwards towards the tenth tee.

'Firstly then I want you to show me that you will not escape,' I instruct firmly from behind as he strides ahead confidently.

'How can I show you master?' he turns around and asks eagerly.

'By playing only with this,' I answer pulling out the lob wedge, the most lofted club in his bag, and handing it too him.

His eyes immediately give away the natural sense of disappointment he is feeling. Ahead is a medium length par-four of 360 yards that slopes steeply downhill to the green; and in his mind it is a hole that appears very inviting and welcoming and one that should offer some respite and the chance to sink a decent score. Despite all that has just been said between us; he is still hoping to continue his vein of form and to improve his scorecard over the second half of the course. As is my intention, my offering serves to kybosh these false hopes completely! If he accepts my terms he will be lucky to even get the ball on the green in par let alone in the hole!

He says nothing for he knows that he dare not betray his warm words of deference so soon by reacting in protest. Quietly then he takes the wedge and mutters under his breath in all seriousness:

'Very well then. Not my will but thy will be done.'

To begin with I watch and see how he cannot help but stand there and wrack his mind in order to remember the teachings from the front half of the course in the hope that they will somehow help him to get through this tricky situation. But how little does he know that subtly, ever so subtly, it is these teachings themselves that are going to be the one thing that will bar him from the gate into the kingdom on this back nine. This baggage we have accumulated so far may have served him well to get to this gate; but I will soon have to break the news that there is nothing from his recent and not -so-recent past that will serve him through these coming holes. For now though I must bide my time and simply watch and wait for the right moment to come...and to let this error of thought play itself out.

So he turns to his breathing to steady himself and he turns to the teachings from the sixth and seventh to make sure that he doesn't try to force the shot in order to eek out those extra precious yards. It is beautiful to see how well he is able to play the part of the straight and pious golfer now in holding his patience and poise to play the most true and perfect wedge off the teeing area. With discipline and focus he has let go of his attachments to the outcome and has simply played the shot before him on its merit. Bravo!

But even this is not enough for him. As he walks after his shot I can observe that he is not merely content with trying to take his baggage with him through the gate; he is even trying to impress me, the gatekeeper, with its contents. I watch and observe it all happen; all the ways he is trying to prove to me that he is worthy enough to come back out here onto this part of the course. He is trying so hard to convince me that he deserves the key to the kingdom because he can happily bear to play this hole with a mere lob wedge!

So as he comes to where his opening shot rests he stands there with that whole fake goofy smile etched upon his face and approaches the ball with the same quirky little routine that he simply has to go through each time. All I want to do is to burst out laughing to try and snap him out of these superstitious rituals. He

143

has become so attached to the teaching from the front nine that he fears my disapproval if ever he should sway from it for an instant. Does he know what he is trying to do here and why?

On the one hand this is the hole of the seeker who thinks that he must go through these little rituals; to light his candles, to repeat his mantras and prayers, and to go to his Sunday service at his special little church; before his God will deem him worthy to be spoken to. But if only these seekers would stop for just one moment and *listen* then they would quickly realise that their God is in fact right there speaking to them all the time. Stopping then is the only condition guarding the entrance to the kingdom and there is simply nothing that needs to be done to prove oneself worthy of receiving the key. But he has taken my instruction of '*show me now that you will not escape*' and skipped right on past it. He has done this because from the mind's perspective stopping is the one thing that it simply cannot *do.*

And then on the other hand this hole can also turn into the martyr's final resting place. For the tenth can easily turn into a graveyard for lost souls who become literally *wedged* between two worlds like a record stuck in a groove. Human history is well littered with these wandering ascetics and suffering saints who walk around wearing t-shirts that have '*I played the tenth with a wedge*' printed upon the back. I know these lost mortals well and the ways in which they love to show how much personal hardship they are prepared to go through in order to gain access to God's innermost chamber. Their capacity to endure endless suffering gives them some strange puffed up feeling of specialness…but unless they snap out of this mindset; it will sadly lead them no further in their game than here. They too are not prepared to stop and listen.

Whilst all this is going on in my mind; another two perfect wedges have been struck down the middle of this hole and he will now have a decent chance of getting the ball on the green with his fourth shot. I watch as he turns towards me anxiously just to check whether I am watching and totting up all his merit points he has earned along the way. I simply gave a big yawn back in return which must have left him utterly baffled as to whether he is playing it right!

How utterly beguiling it seems to the human mind that the teachings themselves are the things that may have helped bring him to the gate but are the very things that are going to stop him from going any further beyond this tenth hole because he is using them as a means to escape the moment. Deep down I see the way that his mind thinks. I see him thinking that even though he may not be able to direct the flow of water down the mountainside; if he at least manages to stay in the water and honour the process, it will at least bring him to the sea at some point in time.

This tenth hole serves to blow that whole agenda apart because I can see how he still believes that there is somewhere better to be than right here on this hole and with this lob wedge in hand. Deep down he is still trying to find a way to use the teachings to get somewhere other than where he is right NOW.

So the game rumbles on because the time is still not yet ripe for me to intervene. He is only 90 yards shy of the green; but I am correct in my prediction that it will be tough to get on the green in par as his fourth shot catches the breeze and sails slightly short and wide to the right. Without a putter to play with, I know he will also be challenged to get the ball in the hole once it is upon the putting surface; and so it proves as it takes him a further four stumbling shots with the wedge's face to send the ball tumbling down into the cup.

Now the hole has been completed it is time to see whether he reveals himself to be the seeker who hopes to give the wedge straight back…or the martyr who prefers to hold onto it for a little while longer. Barely a second passes before he reveals his true colours as he picks the ball out of the hole and offers me back the wedge in the same movement…giving it to me as if it was a burning rod of iron that he could handle no longer.

By doing so the good news is that, unlike the martyr, he can at least complete the tenth hole. The bad news though is that, unbeknownst to him, he has now just set himself up for an even bigger fall on the eleventh.

For now though he is standing there pleading with me to answer the prayer of devotion he has just been practicing down the tenth and is asking me to turn this burning hot wedge into gold. He was in a non-too-subtle way telling me; *I must have surely arrived at the sea by now.*

'Mark that eight on your card,' I reply sharply bringing him back to the moment.

He immediately blushes in embarrassment for he knows instinctively that he has just been caught out for being too wilful. Deep down he'd been hoping to sweep that whole embarrassing and humiliating experience away under the carpet and to move quietly on without another murmur. But with just those six words I'd pulled him back and had given him a clear glimpse into his habit of escaping the moment.

It wasn't quite enough to crack through his mind's defences completely; but it was enough to cause him to fall silent and to not utter a further word as he scribbled that eight down on his card as I have asked.

A Crucifixion

I pointed him towards the path that wound itself through the trees and out to the eleventh tee beyond. There waiting for us was a daunting par five that stretched out down a narrow tree-lined fairway which swept gently around in a crescent shape to a big opening which held the green at its heart. Fierce pot bunkers were scattered throughout like minefields and I knew from experience that any ball that found one would struggle to make par down here.

As we walk together I turn my head and look upon him with mournful eyes. He has not asked me again to take the wedge from his hands but I know that as soon as his eyes fell upon the long hole ahead that his troubled mind was holding out for some sort of a reprieve. Why are my eyes so mournful you may wonder?

There is sadness here for I know that the one beside me is at heart a kind, just and virtuous man who does seek good in the world. Though it is clearly still laced with hidden agendas; he has now become obedient to something higher than the everyday self-ish concerns of lesser men. He has proved to me in coming this far that he is pious and a willing seeker of all that is true. So why can this be not enough to satisfy the one who demands much more than piety and why as his guide do I now have to turn the screw even tighter upon him?

It is a troubling question but this is the way things have always been for the rare souls who have ever reached this point in the game. Like in the biblical story of Job, it is simply not enough that he be good and virtuous in manner. Providence must now

147

intercede to test this man to the fullest so that there is nothing left inside to block the flow of divine grace coming through him. Let me be clear that everything, absolutely everything, of this man that stands in its way – both the good and the bad - must now go.

'You can give me back your wedge now,' I finally give my instruction as we reach the teeing area.

'Oh thank you master,' he answers breathlessly with a new found zest for the game suddenly emerging in his eyes. In an instant I can see his mind already jumping ahead and envisioning where to strike his drive.

'You must play with this instead,' I respond by placing the wedge in the bag and offering him the putter in return with my outstretched hand.

He looks at me completely aghast.

'You can't expect me to play this hole with just a putter. That's sheer madness!'

Much as I expected he is balking at my request for whenever the putter is offered it will be instantly rejected because it goes against the deepest primal instinct for survival. We may go around being just and pious all we like…but when it comes to the crunch it is not enough to stop us going for the throat whenever that survival is threatened. The offer of the putter is simply a humiliation that crosses the line of all reasonableness. But it is however the cross that he must now bear. It is his destiny.

'I asked you to not escape from what is right here in the present moment no matter what it is,' my words come back firm and fair.

'But have I not got better things to do with my time and energy than playing the game with *that*,' he points accusingly at the object in my hand that he is still refusing to take. 'It will be the death of me,' he adds melodramatically.

'Let it be said upfront that human history is full of tales of great men and women who spent the best part of their lives dedicated to something that had no obvious meaning, value, or purpose to it; often dedicating themselves to a vision that seemed quite bizarre and unreasonable...even to themselves...but who nevertheless did it because this is what they were called to do with their life. They are the ones who did it without expectations or hope but who did it because they had surrendered into playing the game on my terms. They are the ones who lived their lives in ignominy in the company of men but who ultimately became elevated into greatness through their trials.'

'But why ruin the game to get us there? Do you know how ridiculous I will look if anyone sees me out here trying to play with *that* club! It's insane that's what it is.'

'It is what it is. I am not asking you to enjoy or be enthusiastic about playing this hole with a putter. But can you just accept and make peace that this is what needs to be done?'

He pauses for a moment to consider my question before reacting angrily.

'No I can't possibly accept such madness. When I came back out here I didn't expect to have my game ripped to pieces like this. The wedge I could just about tolerate but not this. It's just not fair.'

And there it was; the whole fairness word that had reared itself before back on the sixth hole. Then it was not fair that the wind had started to blow and now it was not fair that his guide was asking him to do something that he didn't like. When it came to it he was still behaving like a little child who needed his world to run on his terms and who would throw a tantrum if it didn't. He was still not yet ready to surrender his illusions of control despite all those sweet and earnest words he'd uttered back on that tenth tee.

'What did you say to me on the tenth? Was it something about not betraying my terms and about your longing to complete the course? Now I never promised to you that it would be fair or not; it just is. So why are you making such a big song and dance about it? Now take the putter and get on with it as best you can. Or are you really going to betray me now?'

He falls silent and begins to understand what he has only

brought upon himself. This is a critical moment for his conscience is stirring. Lesser mortals do not dwell here because they can refuse the invitation with the excuse of ignorance and of not knowing any better. Lesser mortals can duck out of the way of the spotlight because they would not dare make the kind of promise that he himself made so boldly back on the tenth. But he cannot duck. To take the putter may be a humiliation but it is surely preferable to resistance which would be a hypocritical step that would lead him to the worst kind of hell.

He is left then in a quandary because without the shield of ignorance he can't find a valid reason to take the putter and he can't find a valid reason to refuse it. His mind has been left completely flummoxed in its wake. This is the struggle of conscience within that everyone has to go through on this eleventh hole because the desire for self preservation is so strong. To fall into a dark abyss without the promise of a divine hand to catch us is truly the strongest act of faith we can ever make.

And though this fall serves to reveal the greatness of the human spirit; it is not a fall that is taken without a lot of resistance in the beginning. Even Jesus shook his fist at the Lord when told to bear the cross and to go through his own crucifixion.

'No I won't betray you master,' he says quietly.

'Oh I am sure you will,' I reply casually; dismissing his solemn stubborn words of devotion.

'How can you say such a thing after all I've done for you,' he reacts instantly with hackles raised.

'Because I know the way it works around here. Do you want to know too?'

'Go on then tell me,' he replies tersely just to placate me; though I sense not really wanting to hear my answer.

'Well what happens when an object accelerates through space and time?'

He is taken aback by the question and shakes his head as if not knowing what to think in response.

'What happens is that it encounters resistance; or pressure. Now you are that object who is trying to accelerate your learning through this back nine and you will continue to encounter the same resistance and pressure. With each hole we will be putting the foot on the accelerator a little firmer which means a little more resistance and pressure in return. It may appear to come from the outside, or it may appear to come from the inside, but in truth it is one and the same. This pressure will lead you to try every possible way to slow the game down; to slow your learning down in order to release it because at times it will seem unbearable. But I will not relent and at some point that pressure will be so intense and so strong that you will refuse me and you will refuse to complete your game. You will betray me and that fateful hour will soon be upon us.'

'Give me that damn putter then and I'll show you that I'm made of stronger stuff than that!' he suddenly reacts forcefully through gritted teeth and with a glint in his eye as he snatches the putter from my still outstretched hand.

His heroic words sound brave; but I know they are foolish for he still does not respect the limits of his own powers. Though he gave the gesture on the tenth tee, he is still refusing to be humbled and to take the fall he has only set up for himself by coming back out to play this second half of the course. They are the words of his resistance and he is still refusing to stop, to listen and to surrender to thy will. Those gritted teeth of his are only going to make things even harder for him down this eleventh; for resistance to the fall can only breed further suffering and anguish.

So standing there on the eleventh tee with putter in hand he has now firmly entered the dark night of his soul. His faith is in crisis and, despite his heroic war cry, he has lost all passion to play this game because he knows all too well now that it will only lead him to this place of death.

For now though he simply knows no other way than to try again by putting the teachings of the first half of the course into practice and to bear this cross as well as he can. He is still struggling and resisting to stop the bottom from falling out and he is still reluctant to just dive right into the moment. He is still trying to escape from where he is now and is still trying to find a way through to some other more welcoming place. He is still refusing to be vulnerable and to open fearlessly to this experience of death for he does not know the glory and the beauty to be found in the unknown state that lies beyond the mind's reach. As is expected, it is all proving too much to bear.

So he stands alone on the tee trying to figure out his best approach to the hole. Does he tee the ball up or hit it from the ground? And what is his best vision for the shot at hand? I stand there and can see his whole mind ticking as he concocts one strategy after another in order to try and navigate his way through this darkest hour with his head held high. So strong is his resistance that he will not seek my counsel anymore because he has lost all faith in me now as his guide. I am the one who has given him the putter and I am no longer going to be treated as a safe and trusted friend.

He has chosen instead then to stand alone in the darkness and he eventually decides to play the shot off the ground. With a full swing he manages to at least strike the ball…but he takes out a big chunk of earth with it in the process.

This is a significant moment because this huge divot is a symbolic gesture of his endeavour to sabotage himself and his game. It is the mind's last stand of resistance with me. This is so because I have stripped away from him all forms of control that he once believed he had. But there is one last form of control that I cannot possibly take from him and which he must eventually relinquish; and that is the power to sabotage everything and to stay stuck here in the darkness of this eleventh hole with only putter in hand. His only power is to dig ever deeper divots into a cavernous pit that he will eventually disappear into.

Seeing him like this reminds me of what I said to him way back on the second hole; when I told him that he had no choice whether to play the game or not…and that his only choice was to sabotage it all so that it all takes a little longer to work his way through. Though he doubted me at the time, he must realise now, without a shadow of doubt, that I can give him the script to perform on stage and he can't possibly wriggle his way out of it. All he has in his power is to perform the script badly, muck everything up, and to try and close his ears to the instructions from an increasingly irate director. He is using the threat of sabotage to try and blackmail me into easing up on him and to give him a better part to play or a happier script to perform. Now standing on stage under the glare of the spotlight, taking a huge divot is the only way he has left to resist my terms.

Though it is all so painful for me to watch, I do quite understand that there is simply no one on this earth who will willingly play the par-five eleventh with only a putter, and that this resistance is all happening in the manner it is meant. Not even a martyr would accept and wear the t-shirt that said '*I played the eleventh with a putter*'...and that, truthfully, is why they themselves can go no further than the tenth.

The eleventh hole is always going to be the toughest hole to play on this course. But play this part he must and silently I cannot relent...even if he so chooses to stay here in this hell for a long, long time. Like a recurring nightmare then we go through the whole routine again and again and I can do nothing but stand back and watch him ploughing on with the hole...and also ploughing up the course as he, deliberately in my opinion, fails to work out how to strike a true ball with the putter blade from a full swing.

Then when the ball bobbles its way into one of those pot bunkers it rapidly descends into an absolute farce! It is an improbable shot to try and lift the ball out onto greener pastures but through one last force of his will he is going down there to try anyway. He is literally burying his head in sand as he not only tries once, but two, and then three times to get the ball out. Finally, when it brings no success, this now matured warrior manages to stop himself and to weigh up his options in order to try a different strategy. He takes a penalty stroke and drops the ball out of the back of the

153

bunker. But with the next strike he simply chops the ball wildly into the same pot bunkers face and he is back where he started! With a huff he takes another penalty stroke and tries again...this time more successfully.

Whilst all this is taking place I can say nothing; for I know my advice is not welcomed...and all I can do is watch the horror show and to tot up the rapidly increasing number of strokes he is taking.

By the time he finally gets to the putting surface the count is at twenty-three strokes. The hole is close and he now has no reason to sabotage the process by taking a divot into the smooth flat surface. Suddenly in this moment I watch as panic begins to set in for he realises that the final hour is here. I can see that he is somewhat torn between the relief of liberation that sinking the ball into the cup will bring on the one hand...and the annihilation of death it will bring on the other. Right to the last he is refusing to perform the final crucifying blow from his putter's blade and to bring this hole to its grim conclusion. Four further strikes it takes then before the ball finally gravitates downwards into the darkness of the cup and he falls swiftly to his knees as a broken and hollow man.

'I can't take any more of this. I'm through!' he screams the final death scream of the one who has been well baked by the game.

However, though this clarion call utters the sound of surrender; only I know the difference between giving up as a control ploy and true surrender...and these words are not it. We have come to the mind's last stand and suicide is the ultimate and final act of sabotage that he has left at his disposal. Having folded all the other cards this is the one he is stubbornly refusing to let go of and his death scream is the most desperate attempt at blackmail in order to be free of this nightmare. If I don't intervene we both know that he will be kept bound here for a long time on this eleventh green with putter in hand and ball resting asleep in the cup. It will not be a pretty fate.

'Pull the plug here and you will remain stuck in this hellish place for a long time. Pull the plug and you will torture yourself by replaying this eleventh hole again and again until you figure a way to break free of its repetitive loop. I seriously advise you to consider carefully before deciding to stop here.'

'But how else can I continue! Look at me. I'm a broken man.'

'As long as I say for you to continue you can. There is nothing I have given you that has been impossible to bear. Remember your invocation on the tenth to do thy will. Well thy will is for you to continue.'

Well I wish I'd never come back out onto the course and said that. Looking back now I was perfectly happy back there on the ninth despite what I said. I wish I could forget it all and just go back to the way things were.'

Although I knew they had to come out, these words of his final betrayal still had the power to sting my heart. He catches a glimpse of my disappointment and so he jumps in to try and justify his betrayal with reason.

'Look I know you think that I just want to head back to my comfort zone on the ninth because I am missing all the trinkets that par gave me. But it isn't that at all. I just want to get back to that *state of flow* where I can just enjoy playing my shots and enjoy playing my game. Maybe I can't take the resistance and pressure from this period of acceleration and maybe I have failed you; oh I don't know; whatever. But I just don't know what you expect of me because I am over this whole God damn business of playing these impossible putter shots out of pot bunkers!'

'So you are back to saying; 'my will not thy will be done'. You are saying you want to go back to playing the game on your terms?'

'Well thy will only wishes me to suffer so how can I possibly continue to play on your terms!'

I ignore this last comment. Both of us know deep down that it is his stubborn resistance that is the cause of his suffering here not the pot bunker he found or the putter I have given. However, only one of us dares to admit it. If only he could stop that mind of his for

155

just an instant all that resistance would go and he would no longer have need to tell me his stories and his reasons for he would see them immediately for the illusion that they really are.

I cannot help but reminisce over when he first came here with the freshness of the beginner's mind and had that brief moment of opening back on the first. We both know that this is really what he wants; not the taste of the ninth again. Alas; if only he could stop that mind of his then this rare experience of grace would surely be available to him all the time!

But I know that this is the way it must go out here and that the mind will only come to a final surrendering stop in its own good time. In truth, though his despair sounds ominous, this is all happening as expected for there are few who come off that eleventh green with the sweet serenity of surrender hanging over a silent mind. He still needs to learn for himself that having his world under his control, as he so wishes, gives him no more peace than he is feeling now. No matter how hard he tries to write a happy script for himself; he cannot escape from that and he needs to finally learn for himself that nothing, *absolutely nothing*, that happens to him in his game truly brings him any further or any closer to the genuine experience of grace. Let it be said again that there is no perfect golf shot in this world that he can play to consummate his heart's deepest longing.

'So how do you want to proceed?'

'Well can't you please just ease up on me and give me my clubs back so I can carry on playing and finish the game. Please don't leave me here with this damn putter like this.'

'Is that your only request?'

'Yes, yes, yes,' his eyes light up as he finally thinks that his pleas are being heard.

'Very well here are your clubs,' I answer passing them to him…before walking off in a different direction from the twelfth tee. For the moment he has made his choice and I must now make mine.

'Wait a minute, where are you going!' he shouts after me.

It's funny how he cared not if I was around a few moments ago and now he is suddenly worried that he might have lost something important here.

'I have taught you all I can. Just carry on and use all you have learned from the front nine and you will find that you will be able to make a comfortable life for yourself with your full set of clubs at hand. So go on and forget about me.'

'But how can I complete the game without you?' he cries out desperately.

'You can't…but then again you've just said that you don't want to complete it. You told me what you want and I am giving it to you. What else is there for me to do?'

'I didn't say I didn't want to complete it. I just asked you to ease up on me!'

'It's one and the same thing. Either you surrender to this moment or you don't. There is simply no other way to complete the game.'

He stares after me wide-eyed and utterly baffled by what I am asking. He thinks what I ask is impossible; but in truth it is only impossible to his mind that cannot possibly see where it is I am pointing. I carry on walking and he is left standing there bemused into a stunned silence.

He thinks he has missed his chance with me…but I know what is to come and that this is all unfolding according to plan. The next three holes will show him what it is really like to play the game on my terms and they are designed to corner him gently into an ultimate place of no escape. With only one or two of these holes played he will still have an escape route and so he will need all three before his mind can come to a natural stop. These three holes are going to give him a glimpse into the riddle and the mystery of existence; a glimpse into the non-dualistic paradigm that our small petty minds cannot possibly comprehend or grasp. After the blunt delivery of the eleventh he is going to find the teaching of the coming holes a lot more subtle for the non-dualistic perspective is extremely slippery to comprehend. It is so subtle in fact that I am confident it will slip through his defences and will catch him unawares before this suicidal and desperate saboteur realises what has happened. How little does he know that the tenth and eleventh have all been a necessary set-up for what is now about to come!

The Perfection of Form

In truth I cannot stray far from him, as he moves across reluctantly to the twelfth tee, for I have a duty of care that I can't possibly walk away from. The moment he calls me back I will be there immediately but for now I have to leave him with a visible sense of abandonment following his inevitable act of betrayal.

The hole itself offers a welcome respite for him from all that has come before. It is a par-three of 160 yards in length and the flag flutters invitingly at the back centre of the green. There are no hazards other than a few recently planted trees dotted around the green's edge and it feels a lot more open and inviting than the long and treacherous eleventh. He takes a five iron and for this moment at least it doesn't seem such a bad swap; trading in his soul for the bag of clubs like this. I can see how the freedom to choose and the freedom to play without pressure upon his shoulders suddenly feels quite liberating. Although he has chosen to drop down onto a circular path that just goes around and around the bottom of the mountain; it is at least flatter and easy to walk upon than the vertical ascent of the eleventh.

The effect of his liberation is immediate as he enters the doorway and holds a positive vision. He is immediately rewarded for his full and bold commitment to the iron shot as the ball is sent straight and true like an arrow towards the target. It lands short on the front edge; but the green is hard here and the ball does not come to rest. Instead it rolls onwards and onwards over the putting surface to nestle down within four feet of the hole. It is possibly his most delicious shot of the day; but in looking back to the lone figure standing on the tee I don't see any of the wide-eyed wonder of the first, the seduced dreaminess of the fifth, or the wild fist pumping of the ninth. Instead the only thing I can say is that he just looks utterly relieved to be back again in the groove.

With a newfound enthusiasm for the game he begins to walk jauntily and gives the impression that he no longer has a care in the world. His putter has been tucked snugly under his arm as a proud gesture to show the world that he has found the right target with his tee shot. Oddly enough this is the same putter that only a moment ago he was cussing and cursing with obscenities. Now it seems to have become a trusted friend again because it no longer is associated with me and with my impossible demands. I am truly amazed to see how quickly the scars of the eleventh that are marked on that putter's face have been forgotten and how much resilience he has to bounce back like this. It all shows how well he was trained on the front nine of the course.

I am not hurt though to see him carrying on so well without me for I know that this marvellous reinvention of his spirit has no firm foundations and he will not be able to sustain this soulless life for long. Appearances are deceiving and I just have to bide my time before the cracks begin to appear. This is because once you are out here on the back nine you can no longer go back to your old ways no matter how hard you may try to close your eyes and to cover your ears. Once you have been called to journey forth into the mystery, the door can no longer be closed shut in ignorance. He may like to keep up the pretence but deep down he knows that it is simply not okay to betray his soul like this no matter how many times he goes on to strike a perfect shot. I may have given him the advice to forget about me but I knew full well in saying it that such advice is going to be impossible to heed.

Although it appears then as if the twelfth offers an easier respite from what has come before; I for one know that his suffering is going to be far more acute and far more intense than anything he experienced on the tenth or eleventh. On this twelfth

160

hole he is going to have to learn the hard way that there is no longer going to be a safe pillow for his head to rest upon in the world. This hole then has a horrible haunting quality as the twist in its tale.

For the moment though he is revelling in the hour of ignorance and in the freedom to forget again who I am. The ball is nestled close to the hole and the promise of a first glorious birdie awaits him to be fulfilled. Not that the outcome matters that much to him of course because it is more the experience of flow that he wished for. Coasting along with neither foot on the accelerator or the brake; life seems strangely good and that swagger has returned to his gait as he strides confidently towards the green. He approaches the putt confidently then and without fear.

The ball rolls straight and true towards the hole like a missile honed in on its target and disappears sweetly into the cup to bring about the perfect end to a perfect hole. Without any fuss this is the experience of everything coming simply and neatly together.

But does it really leave a sweet lingering taste? For in the time it took for the ball to drop and for it to land down in the base of the cup; I watch keenly and I see the satisfaction immediately turn bitter in his mouth. I see it all in his expression as his face screws up in sourness. What strange thought was passing through his mind in this moment I wonder? I can guess the answer for flashing right there before him was the image of this perfect putt expanding outwards and outwards right throughout the golf course until it manifested as the most perfect hole and then the most perfect game that passed without a single lapse. And what would that perfect game look like exactly?

Well it would simply be a game of fifty perfect shots of:
drive, iron, putt, drive, iron, putt, drive, wood, putt, iron, putt, drive, iron, putt, drive, wood, putt, iron, putt, drive, iron, putt, drive, iron, putt, drive, iron, putt, drive, wood, putt, iron, putt, drive, iron, putt, drive, iron, putt, drive, iron, putt, drive, wood, putt, iron, putt, drive, iron, putt.

And then after this thought has sunk in, the next thought pictures this perfect game expanding outwards and outwards so that it was replayed again and again all the way to eternity. For with my words still ringing in his ears he knows all too well that he cannot complete and leave the golf course now and so manifesting this fifty shot game over and over is the highest achievement he can possibly squeeze out of it. Unless of course he holes an iron shot or drives the ball 350 yards onto the green of the shortest par four. But this is semantics.

And what was the next thought which seemed to give rise to this critical bitterly sensation in the mouth? Well I am certain that the thought came that though he wanted it now, and would probably enjoy it for a while, in time he would soon get *utterly bored* with the game should he ever happen to realise this perfection he so craves. So bored in fact that in time he would probably want to give up the game for good! In fact he probably has seen there and then that even though the twelfth looks a far better experience to have than the eleventh; both are ultimately *the same* because both eventually bring him to the same gate of suicidal despair; of wanting to give up the game completely. As I had already predicted; neither experience holds the power to bring him ultimate peace.

With this strange thought lingering on I watch and see him stand there looking utterly flummoxed by what is taking place. He seems perplexed by the realisation that this utopian birdie two on the twelfth was leaving him feeling as much despair as a twenty-seven shot horror show on the eleventh.

In this exalted moment he has finally grasped the utter emptiness of this perfect robot golf that he had once wanted for himself. He had a glimpse in the professional shop but now the realisation has been sown deep. In this moment he has realised how much he needs the messiness and chaos of the game that his soul had brought to him. He wanted the variety, the ups and downs, the twists and turns, the good and the bad, the beautiful and the ugly. He wanted it all in his game and did not want to just manufacture one side of the equation through the will of his mind and through the immaculate control of his golf clubs. He wanted the golfing arena that allowed and accepted all this to happen and he begins to remember what was said to him way back on the fourth green when he had the thought of disappearing over the boundary fence into the void. Yes that's right. Back then I had told him that it was only by embracing the vagaries of this game that he could find meaning and purpose within it. Getting in the flow then isn't to do with ironing away all the cracks so that life runs clockwork smooth without a foot out of place. Getting in the flow is simply good advice to help us work the process and challenges that this game inevitably throws our way and to evolve our learning through them. Try and take away those vagaries and his whole mission on this earth will simply fall away to dust. He will have learned nothing and helped no-one in the process.

It was in that moment of revelation that he looked upwards to the heavens and screamed in anguish:

'Can there be no safe place for me to rest in this world!'

Where Magic and Miracles are Found

At the sound of this cry of anguish; my cue has been given and I return once more to his side. I descend from my hiding place in the thick gorse bushes and stride boldly to where he stands alone and adrift on this twelfth green.

'No there is no place to rest peacefully in a mind-created world; no matter how perfectly that world reflects your innermost desires. You know this now.'

I take the putter from his hand and place it into the bag whilst he stands there looking at me with suspicion as if knowing that I have a hand in all of this. It is a look of realisation that once this guide enters your life and stirs your soul that he will never leave you alone. Though I have known it from the very beginning; he has finally realised for himself that ignorance can never now be his tonic of bliss.

He has become silent; like a cornered lamb that has realised that any more struggle is only futile and that there is no possible way of escape. He has accepted his destiny and has fallen limply down at my feet.

'I still don't understand though,' are five simple and honest words that finally come forth from his lips whilst he hovers down by my boot soles.

'Then that means you are now ready for the truth,' I answer firmly pointing him towards the thirteenth tee; and then lovingly picking him up to his feet.

Though an unlucky number for some, I cannot help but say beforehand that the thirteenth is without a doubt my favourite hole on the course. This is the hole where anything is possible and it is where magic and miracles are awaiting the one who has surrendered his will to thine. This is going to be a potent hole of revelation that will take him far beyond his wildest dreams.

He doesn't know this yet of course for his eyes have become too cast down by events. The one who comes to the thirteenth hole has been walking through a desert for a long, long time and it is not surprising that he has given up hope of finding water. He has enough faith to keep on walking but no longer does he anticipate the fairytale ending of the golden oasis appearing like a conjuring trick. Parched dry by his struggles, there is no spark of joy to be found anywhere out here.

As the thirsty man only wishes for water; the one who comes to the thirteenth hole knows that the illumination of divine grace is the only thing that can now satisfy him. This is all that he wants and as his cup has been emptied to the bottom the time is ripe for it to be filled to the brim so that he may quench this thirst. The twelfth didn't do it but the thirteenth will and I promise that by this hole's end he will be so saturated with this grace that he will not need to go thirsty again. Now that his mind has gotten out of the way; he will soon see the full extent of divine power working in and through him and will see it charging his life with new and unimaginable possibilities. Very soon he will get a lasting taste of what this whole arduous journey of surrender has been for.

The thirteenth appears to be a tough par four and according to the scorecard it is ranked as the hardest on this back nine; and the third toughest on the course. Its length is its greatest challenge for two long and accurate shots are required to find the putting surface. There is also a small brook that runs alongside the right hand side marking the far boundary of the course; and there is a thick clump of trees lined up all the way down the left. Between these a tight fairway cuts its way through the middle where the white flag can just be seen in the far distance.

The tee shot is a daunting one to play even for a golfing expert, and I for one am not surprised to see his club wobble here.

Wary of going out of bounds to the right; he lets his drive slide off away into the trees to the left. We hear the clatter of wood but though it appears as if it was the fear of error that truly caused this wobble; I know deep down that this is all the hand of destiny at work. For although the mind thinks that keeping it straight is essential to navigate this hole successfully; I was anticipating this loose shot because the time is ripe for me to show the power of the unorthodox. Deep into the wilderness is the way we are meant to go down here because he needs to see that though we try hard to steer clear of the rough in our game; sometimes there are great treasures to be found when one follows the unconventional path towards the green and the cup. It is time for us to go further into the paradox and the mystery.

His silence remains deep as we walk off together as his mind no longer has any power to step in and judge the situation. After what has just happened to him on the eleventh and twelfth he can no longer say with any conviction what is right and what is wrong. All distinctions have blurred together and his mind is left spinning in the grey fog that has descended and swiftly suffocated all rules of reason. He remains expectant but he is no longer searching, no longer waiting, and no longer trying to prove himself worthy of anything. These are all sure signs that he is ready for the firework show to begin.

We easily find his ball perched up on some loose twigs and leaves. There is plenty of space under these mature deciduous trees to swing the club but if any height is put on the shot then it is liable to smack against wood. Ideally he will want to play a flat shot so that the ball only rises a foot or so off the ground. Not only that but the trunks of the trees ahead also present a challenging obstacle to navigate past in order to bring the ball out onto open ground.

He ponders the shot to play and slowly pulls a three iron from the bag. He has a clear impression of the shot he wants to play here and the iron he strikes is a pure one. However, whilst its trajectory remained low enough; its accuracy was not perfectly true as it clipped the left hand side of the last remaining tree trunk thirty yards ahead and the little white ball was sent spinning back into trouble. I turn towards him and the only flicker of emotion he showed in return was a raised eyebrow. It was almost an apologetic gesture as if somehow he still has the lingering feeling that he has let me down with the way he is playing out here.

We walk on to where the ball has come to rest and it is clear that this will be an even trickier shot to play with even more obstacles to navigate through. The ball is also nestled down among leaves and twigs and so it is going to be tough to get it out whilst keeping the trajectory as low as the last shot. There are 160 yards to go from here to the flag and it appears to be an almost impossible shot to play in order to get the ball anywhere near the green. Despite the difficulty we can both see the one precise shot that would do it. He would have to play a low snap hook that would bend itself right around the obstacles ahead and out towards open ground. To actually bring the ball to rest on the green itself is probably a one-in-a-hundred shot to pull off.

The sacred hour is upon us and I feel the same electricity that was in the air when he first stumbled across that gate way back yonder. The atmosphere is being saturated with pregnant possibility and as the ancient Greeks would have said; we are entering again into kairos time. I notice the light beginning to change with the path ahead looking more luminous and iridescent with each passing moment. I looked across sharply to see if he could see it too but his perception clearly wasn't yet vibrating at that level. But his faith must at least be strong because help was definitely at hand from those who come to serve as messengers from the higher realms. Angels, dakinis, devas; you may call them what you will, but their presence is a sure sign that something incredible is about to happen here. I can feel their grace descending to lift him up to new higher levels of expectancy and so the sense of anticipation is tantalising me. Out here in the untamed wilds, nature spirits too have appeared to watch in curiosity and to lend their own encouraging voice to the ensemble. Even the trees have paused for breath to witness what is taking place. He is being mightily blessed.

I step in, put my arms around his shoulders and say just four simple words that echoed the potency of the moment whilst he hovered there over the shot ahead of him.

'It can be done.'

'So be it,' he answers after I step back and he swings the three iron back and through in a completely open and ready state to receive the inspiration of this descending grace upon him. He is flooded with light and everything comes together sweetly in a momentary flash upon impact of club on ball. The deliberate snap hook has guided his ball out and around the obstacles and we run out together to get a glimpse of it bounding merrily along the fairway. It goes and it goes and it goes; getting closer and closer to the green all the while. Just when it seems to be coming up short there is a little dip in the ground that gives it the extra momentum to carry it all the way onto the front of the green about twenty feet shy of the flag! He has just pulled off his very first miracle!

The smile on his face is so broad and full and I have never seen him looking as content as he is right now. It is true that he had a beginner's taste of this way back on the first; but let's remember that back then he wasn't as thirsty as he is now and there just wasn't so much room in his cup to be filled. And though that was a marvellous shot; it wasn't as improbable as this one was. He turns across and looks at me in bewilderment and it is as if in the midst of this heady contented state he is suddenly struck by the absurd parody of the situation.

'How can it be that I feel so much more satisfied and joyful out here in the rough than I ever felt playing my perfect straight shots from the fairway?'

'This joy does not come to you from space or time but only right here in this present moment. It matters not where you have been or where you are going to. It matters not also whether you are on the fairway or in the rough. There is simply no place where it cannot be found in the here and now.'

'But why does this joy appear so much more vivid and alive

here in these trees.'

'It is only because on the fairway your mind thinks it is master; and when your mind is in charge you miss it. Only out here in the deep rough is there elbow room for me and all the other heavenly forces to get to work and to reveal to you the immense power of divine grace within your life. As you can see, when you let go, anything is possible and there are no limits to the powers of creation that you have at hand.'

'Other heavenly forces?' he asks looking around in puzzlement. 'Am I not alone here down here with you?'

'Do you really think you could have pulled that shot off under your own steam?'

'Well I had the vision of the shot I wanted to play like you taught me on the ninth. I was the one who created it,' he answers boldly.

'Okay then do it again,' I respond throwing a ball on the ground in the same spot. He looks back at me hesitantly.

'You can't expect me to pull it off every time can you?'

'If you are the creator here then why can't you?'

'Okay I get your point,' he answers humbly no longer wishing to resist by giving it a shot. 'There was a bit of luck in there too,' he admits sheepishly.

'So it was as much to do with luck as judgment. Well tell me what does luck mean to you?'

'Something like a kind bounce or a favourable roll I guess.'

'And is it not at all possible that, even though you can't see it, there could be other forces at work here to bring these moments of luck about?'

'You mean angels and stuff like that,' he answers sceptically.

'You are not yet sensitive enough to perceive these angelic forces but your faith is at least strong now for them to come to your aid whenever you are in trouble and to bring about more of these moments of 'luck'. Like me, these beings are here to help guide you through the obstacles before you. You really couldn't have pulled off that shot without them.'

'But no-one believes in that stuff nowadays and yet some people live with a lot of luck in their lives.'

'It doesn't take your belief to make them real. And those who get a favourable rub of the green may not speak of angels but if you take a closer look you will see they do speak the language of faith. It is faith that brings about the miracle here.'

'But the guy who keeps his ball out of the rough doesn't need faith does he. To me the lucky break sounds like a comforting thing to hold onto whenever we stumble in this world. Surely it is not the ideal?'

'It is the nature of things that man will find the rough sometimes and so faith is not to be a luxury or to be the sustenance of the poor. Faith must surely come first in your life.'

'But why must something go wrong before something can go right? Why must I play the bad shot first before I can get the chance to play the great recovery?

'That's all part of the mystery of this world and of this life. Why is it that if you started to play the perfect game of golf that you would give it up in an instant? Why is it that the only thing that gets you out of bed and out on the course is the possibility of playing just that one shot in your game that leaves you utterly struck with awe? This is all part of the human dilemma of existence. We come and in the midst of the mundane flux of our lives we all long for something that touches us and proves that there is some higher force here at work behind the screen. This is faith and in return it brings us these moments of joy that give our lives genuine meaning. Now look into your heart and tell me what doorway you have been using in your practice? Is it the feeling of a straight laced shot when you were in complete control or is it something less conventionally perfect?'

'You are right! To begin with on the ninth tee I did try and connect with that sweet iron I struck on the fifth…but when I went into my heart there was nothing inside. It was a shot utterly bereft of substance. Strangely the shot I connected with next was the lob wedge I'd just taken back on the eighth. It was a shot that was completely spontaneous and unorthodox and one that totally fuelled my imagination. It is a shot that makes my heart sing just feeling into it again now.'

'A mundane hole transformed into life,' I muse in agreement.

'So you are saying that there are these invisible forces that helped me to pull that shot off?' he asks intrigued by the idea.

'Whenever you are in your heart and playing with faith then you will always be encouraged,' I answer cryptically.

'It's strange but coming out here with you I had the impression that perfecting my game would bring me more joy and satisfaction. I believed it would get me further in the game and give me more success. Yet feeling like this now I can't believe that that impression once had its hold over me. It seems ridiculous thinking about it now especially when I look back at my favourite golfing memories. My heroes were not the plodders who went about carving up the course like robots. I mean, who remembers the champion who needs a par down the eighteenth and who goes solidly from tee to fairway to green and two straight putts? My favourite memories through history are of those are of players who somehow pulled off the miraculous recovery shot at the most important moment in a tournament. I think recently of Bubba Watson and his ridiculous shot out of the trees on the tenth at Augusta; or Tiger Woods chipping in there on the sixteenth. These moments almost seemed destined.'

'It is easy to admire the destined hour when you see it happen to others; but because these moments are rare and uncertain it is a lot harder to live fully by them yourself. We all come out here longing for a life that we can control and that gives us a certain outcome. Though it is not admirable, when it comes to the crunch most wish to play it safe and to choose the path that plodders tread. At first glance this seems to be the only sane way to play the game. But beyond that appearance there is another way to play.'

171

'I see. But are you really telling me that a higher hand was pulling the strings to make it happen?'

'Is that really so incredible to believe? Of course you must realise first that a professional golfer has to practice and practice and to hone and sharpen his game as much as he can to get himself in that position. He must make sure his club doesn't wobble. This is his responsibility. But no matter how much he practices he must at the same time recognise that the defining moments will always come to him from beyond his control and only through his faith.'

'Yes, and going back further, Seve Ballesteros was probably my favourite player to watch because his wholehearted way of playing the game seems to epitomise exactly what you are talking about here. He was a magician with a wedge and I once dreamed of modelling my whole game around pulling off the Seve miracle shot around the greens! How could I have so easily forgotten all of this?'

'That's right. It is important to recognise that you are so magnetised to those unorthodox players who don't play the game with straight and rigid lines but in moments of spontaneous brilliance. They were the ones who inspired you to leave your plodding existence for a new life lived in faith. These are the players who showed to you that the only place where joy and meaning can be found is in the present moment. They are the ones, who come and play the game with character; who come and play the game with the authentic light of their soul shining through. They take risks rather than play it safe and they bring colour and another dimension to the black and white monotony of the mind-controlling golfer. They are the ones who illuminate the paradoxes and mysteries of the game and who embrace the non-dualistic wisdom that is to be found in the here and now.

'These players taught you that these moments of spontaneous genius are the only moments that can bring real purpose to your life. Although they seem to descend at random from nowhere into the hands of both saint and sinner alike; the only determining factor is that they will never fall in the lap of the one who plays the game solely through their controlling mind. But in truth nearly all of us will have had that experience where it feels like the hand of destiny is falling kindly upon our shoulders and deep down we all come and play this game for that one moment when that hand does come to fall upon us. This is the sacred longing that lies within all human beings because in the midst of our ups and downs and in the midst of our often messy and chaotic lives where good and bad things happen; we all want to be touched by the hand of the sacred at least once. We all want the golfing gods to smile down upon us at least once.

'We've spoke about this already down the first when the moment of grace first came in to ignite your interest in the game. But back then your mind was far too busy to really appreciate the moment because it was too busy thinking how to hold onto it and how to recreate it again and again. Now on the thirteenth you are better prepared to simply say thank you for this grace and to let it go, not knowing if she will ever come upon your game ever again. This is what it means to live in faith; and you are ready for it.'

With that the teaching of this hole has been given and he walks on towards the thirteenth green feeling deeply content with his life again. In this moment it feels good to live with faith and courage and with an openhearted expectancy that anything is possible. Once on the green it takes two strikes of his putter to bring the ball to rest in the bottom of the cup and to bring the hole to a close with a bogey five.

The Place of No Return

He comes off the thirteenth green still beaming at what has taken place. The struggles of the tenth and eleventh, and the emptiness of the twelfth, are now but distant memories for the one whose thirst has been so thoroughly quenched. But such is his maturity now that he no longer needs to hold on to the experience for he realises that all he has to do is empty his cup and it will surely be filled again.

This fourteenth hole is a shorter par four; albeit one that doglegs sharply to the right. Three tall oak trees stand as sentinels keeping guard of the dogleg's corner, making it risky to try and cut a few yards off the second shot by taking them on. Deep rough runs to their right and it would take a truly bold shot to try and carry this and to make the fairway beyond it. Playing to the left of the trees with an iron is the safer shot to play from the tee and wisely this is exactly what he is choosing to do as he takes the three iron from the bag.

The shot is true, and though he will have a much longer approach, he has at least got a clear view of the green and a decent lie to play from. It is right here that I know we will come upon the third and final subtle lesson to be learned. He doesn't realise it yet but without this lesson he won't be able to come to the final resting place of surrender before thy will.

So as he stands there over the four iron shot he has left to play, I see it is beginning to dawn on him that the game isn't over yet. For quite suddenly he finds himself in a strange quandary towards the shot he has to play. One eye has fallen upon the green and the hole that sits at its heart. But mysteriously the other eye has fallen upon the deep bank of gorse bushes that run around the back half of the green. I watch all this uncertainty hanging over him and I see how the mind immediately steps back in to provide its own resolution to the dilemma. For his mind well remembers what happened on the thirteenth; and he also well remembers what happened on the twelfth. Now it seems as if he is faced with a choice of which of these two experiences he wishes to recreate. Does he want to hit a nice straight iron into the green...but taste its bitter feeling of emptiness? Or does he want to hit a wild shot into the gorse...and possibly rediscover the magical gift of recovery once there?

These questions are misguided; but they are necessary ones for him to ask on this fourteenth hole. They are misguided because he has already forgotten what I said back on the thirteenth that it matters not whether he finds himself on green or gorse; for grace is to be found in all places and across all time. Although humans throughout history have chosen the way of the cross as the method of getting into thy kingdom; it isn't necessary to come in kicking and screaming like this. Yes heading into the deep rough is the way that mankind has chosen to begin his spiritual path of awakening; the way he has chosen to demonstrate his faith in something that exists beyond the forms of this game through the power of his recovery. But the way isn't exclusive and it is always possible to come in through the gate quietly and at peace.

The only thing that really matters then is that his cup be empty right here and right now.

But he is missing this point for these misguided controlling questions are starting to bung the cup back up. Lured by the prospect of 'doing a Seve', he is now dreamily searching for that grace in the gorse. In thinking this way he is no longer to be found here present in the moment. This goes all the way back to what I mused on the tenth that the one thing the mind cannot do is stop and the one thing it cannot find is the moment. So until his faith is strong enough to hold dominion over that mind he will forever be compelled to miss the ultimate truth that stands before him right now.

Confusedly then he is starting to become identified with the unorthodox existence and the chaotic and messy way of life. By the power of persuasion of his mind he is ready to abandon all of his training of how to be a straight laced golfer because he now thinks that the two paths are mutually exclusive. From his experiences of the last two holes he now holds the stubborn thought that the form and the essence of this game are distinct. Soon he will have to realise the folly of this thought for all is one and grace is in all things.

For now though confusion has its reign over his heart. He seems unable to bring both eyes into focus on the green and one keeps on wandering and wandering into the gorse. He is quivering and it is no wonder that as he strikes the ball in this state of mind that the ball ends up flying exactly as his thoughts intended and bounds wildly through the green and into the wilderness beyond. Alas though he doesn't seem at all disappointed by the result of the shot, and nonchalantly he begins to walk forward.

'Are you not going to play a provisional ball?' I ask, halting him immediately in his stride.

He seems bemused by my question as if struck by the realisation that I am not quite going along with his mind's cunning little plan of seeking exaltation from within the gorse. My words come like a pin prick in his bubble of expectancy.

'What do you mean?' he asks firmly.

'That's a horrible spot where your ball has gone. I wouldn't hold out on finding it so easily if I were you,' I answer bluntly.

He looks at me almost outraged by my words. I am the guide who only a few moments ago was saying that anything was possible with a little bit of faith and now to him I am the one giving a faithless statement of doubt!

'Miracles can happen,' he responds; stubbornly refusing to accept the facts.

'You must understand that faith can never be unreasonable or misty eyed. It must always be grounded in the truth of the moment.'

'It can be found,' he simply replies firmly; echoing back to me my own confident words to him on the thirteenth that it could be done. However, whereas mine were intuited, his are intellectually foolish.

'Very well,' I reply without protest picking up his bag and following behind as he walks ahead confidently. I say no more for I know full well that this is the way the hole must go.

We come to the place where his ball had bounded in, and as I predicted, the gorse is thick and unyielding. It is also prickly and he is getting more and more scratched as the search becomes ever more frantic. He is no longer as thirsty as he was for he is too busy searching and searching for his ball to stop and receive the blessing of this moment. The golf ball has now become his only means of salvation. Without it his folly will be revealed and he will have to record a 'no-return' upon his scorecard; leaving his game incomplete and unfulfilled. The thought of this begins to leave him increasingly desperate and he begins to whimper for illumination and begs for guidance from anyone who may be listening to him. But of course he gets no response and so his brittle faith begins to disappear once more into a state of crisis.

He is getting no response because he is holding out his cup and demanding it to be filled; he is asking rather than listening. So all the while the heavenly forces simply laugh back at him hysterically. As a chorus they cry down to him: *if you want your cup to be filled then you have to empty it first!*

I walk over and stand close by his side whilst putting my arms around his jittery shoulders. '*Stop the search*,' are the three simple words of command that I utter in this tender moment and fortunately, ever so fortunately, he hears them for the very first time and he stops before me like he has never stopped before. He stops because these last three holes have been designed to form together a golden triangle that when completed offer no other way out but to stop. In seeing him surrendered like this, I cannot help but say the words of an ancient sutra that expresses the heart of this non-dual teaching I have been giving:

'Form is emptiness
Emptiness is form
Form is not other than emptiness
Emptiness is not other than form'

He looks at me awestruck with the power of these words for they have served to flummox the mind into utter and complete silence. Everything about these three holes then has been designed to turn the world of duality upside down and let it be said that whatever he thinks it is it is not. Now he finally knows without a shadow of doubt that his mind simply cannot touch upon the mystery of the present moment.

In that moment his cup has been emptied even more deeply and he is ready to be flooded once more with light. After all his efforts and all his struggles to get here; the moment of stopping seems so simple and insignificant an event. And that is the whole point; it is so simple that it is all too easily dismissed! But having now seen he will never not see again for as the scorecard will now forever remind him…this is the hole where he has reached the eternal place from which there can be '*no return*' into dualistic thought. In this moment he has finally awakened fully from the dream of mind.

The Royal Court

T he fifteenth is what is known as the signature hole; the one that defines this course as individually distinct from any other. It is the special hole then that has been lavished with all of the designer's attention to it in order to make it the most uniquely beautiful of them all. We have truly arrived now at the kingdom of heaven and he is firmly ready to enter the gate and to dive into the banquet that is on offer within this royal court.

The hole itself is a par four that is quite short in length. Like the last it has another sweeping dogleg; but this time it goes around almost at right angles to the left hand side. The direct line to the green from the teeing area is almost impossible to take, however; apart from a few brave souls who dare risk it for a large pond stretches out almost from tee to green. The fairway skirts around this vast expanse of water and at the halfway point a brook connects the large pond on the left to a smaller one on the right. Over this small brook spans the most lavishly designed bridge; which is like something out of a magical fairytale. The green itself is small and nestled with trees all around its sides and with three of the most beautifully shaped bunkers you will ever see spanning the front and the right hand sides.

This hole is a celebration for me as my work has been completed and there is nothing for me to say or do to help him down this royal parade. A deep and spacious silence has fallen upon us both and he is ready now to receive the full blessing of divine grace without restraint. He has no more resistance and no more questions to ask. There are no more struggles and grappling with the dualistic world that he has come through these last few holes. There are no more of these ruminating thoughts of *'if it is not quite this then it must be that…and if it is not quite that then it must be this.'* The self has surrendered into the mysteries of the non-dualistic paradigm and he has entered the void. All is unknown in this place and yet at the same time all is possible.

In truth there is not a lot more to report about what happens down here. Grace is a humble and subtle force that moves through and works simply without any of the drama of all our previous holes together. It is a force that moves beneath the radar quietly to serve the greater good; unnoticed and without any undue fuss. Things happen here but there is no self left to try and control it or to take any credit for it. This may be a beautifully carved hole in the landscape but it is certainly not brash or pretentious.

Although there is no interesting story for the mind to tell of what happened down this hole; for posterity's sake let it be said that he came off that fifteenth green with his third par of the game to be recorded upon his scorecard.

A Drop in Vibration

'T hat was lovely,' he remarks to me in a dreamy tone as we walk away from towards the sixteenth tee together.

'Yes it *is* lovely isn't it,' I remark; subtly bringing him back to the moment lest he should falter here much in the way he faltered way back on the first. The flickering flame is now steady in his heart but he must continue to keep it fanned with the spark of his presence. He must never look back at what has been. Always now. Always now.

But instead he misses my beat and skips straight through from past to future with the next words that come: 'Does the game not finish here though?'

This is the question that inevitably comes from the one who has tasted the Kingdom within. With a worried frown he has suddenly done the maths and realised that there are, apparently, still three holes left to play. The clubhouse is in sight ahead of us but there is one last turn outwards into the far yonder and back before the game is done. There is to be one last twist for this golf course is not going to bring the fairytale ending. In this non-dualistic paradigm there is in truth no beginning and no end to the game we are playing and the dance will continue as long as the music is playing.

'The question is not whether you can hold on to what was given but whether you can keep the pot empty so that it may be filled again and again without pause.'

'I see master,' he answers; instantly understanding what I

181

mean. 'Will you show me how I am to keep this pot empty?'

'Circumstances over these three holes will show you,' I answer mysteriously.

'But why can't you master?'

'I am not meant to play these holes leading you by the hand for they are designed to prepare you for your return to an outside world where you will feel alone and unaccepted at times. It is time for you to go back to a world that thinks and acts in completely different ways to you and is up to you now to hold the faith and vision you have realised. You are strong enough.'

'But what is the vision?'

'Do you remember your promise I reminded you of back on the second?'

'Vaguely...but can you remind me again exactly what that was?'

'I said back then that you are the one chosen to come down in order to take on your share of the collective unconscious with the task of transforming it with the light of your consciousness. You are the one chosen to bring spirit into matter rather than separate spirit from matter. You are the one chosen to reveal the light of the Divine through the world of forms and to help advance the evolution of consciousness on this planet by becoming a channel for grace. All of your training thus far has prepared you for this. Now it is time to go forth and *live* it. This is the vision.'

'You really think I am ready now for all of that?'

'Not yet. But by the time you work your way through these next three holes you may be ripe to give it a shot,' I respond mischievously.

'But I don't see why you can't be there, master,' he answers suddenly feeling vulnerable by the prospect of going it alone.

'Because as I said in the very beginning; I cannot come into your world and you cannot come into mine. Your work is outside of these gates in a land where I cannot go. But do not fear for you must realise that you are never truly alone out there. Separation is but a veiled illusion and so remember what happened to you on the 13th and never lose faith in what you now know to be true. And also remember that anytime you feel you have lost your way that this halfway house will always be here to help put you straight again. Just look within your heart and you will find me again.'

'I'll remember,' he says tenderly as I place a fatherly arm around his shoulders.

'Yes I know you will. But please don't be complacent for you will be sorely tested over these remaining holes and there will be a lot of pressure on you to forget. There is room for you to stumble but I promise that you will never fall irrevocably. It is safe for you to go and play.'

'So I really can't stay here and I must return to the outside world?'

'Yes it is your destiny. Once upon a time many enlightened souls did call it a day at the fifteenth and stayed in this heavenly kingdom for eternity. But this is not enough for your generation. The world needs your wisdom and your presence and you must see your promise through until every soul has come through the golf course and tasted the sweet taste of the fifteenth for themselves. You are to be the shepherd of the flock who comes from the rear and not the front.'

'Very well master. If that is so then let it be.'

With an outstretched hand I gesture him towards the sixteenth tee whilst I carry on walking out over the boundary fence and into the wilderness that is my home. I know I will be called upon again and again over the holes to come; but I finally feel relaxed about giving him the space to swing his club now.

The sixteenth hole is the last par five on the course and it is one that rises up to a crest from the tee; before descending down-wards towards the green. The boundary fence I have crossed runs tightly along the right hand side but the fairway is generous and the rough is only light on the left. In many ways it appears to be a rather quaint and gently pottering hole through which he can reintroduce and ease himself gradually back into the ways of the outside world and to explore how to bring his gifts of wisdom to bear within it.

So I watch from afar as he stands there alone on the sixteenth tee and he plays a lovely looking draw shot into the breeze that is blowing from the left; a draw shot that is so perfectly balanced against its opposing force that it keeps the ball straight and true down the fairway. He is so thoroughly attuned to the flow of the elements now that I cannot help but give a little jig in celebration. Grace is now moving and turning the wheel of his life freely at its own will and without any restraint.

I watch as he begins to soar up that slope; naively unaware that the glorious moment will swiftly pass and that a big, big surprise awaits him once he reaches the crest of the fairway on which his ball is nicely perched. Once there he can see what I see; a slow moving four ball that have suddenly appeared about one-hundred yards ahead of him down the slope.

'What the hell; where have they come from...and what on earth are they doing down there?' he exclaims aloud in annoyance.

This surprise has come to him as a complete shock because until now he has been utterly alone on this course. His reaction of course is very revealing as to where he is at in his practice. It is as if someone has just suddenly rudely impinged on his own pleasant little solitary retreat.

The question is rhetorical and I assume it is being directed into the wilderness where I am watching. However, I remain silent in reply. It is not that I don't know the answer but more that I find the question to be frankly irrelevant. Why should he care about the what's and the where's? Who is he to hold judgment over what is happening? But though I am terse in my silence, I do concede that the question is at least an understandable reaction given the jolting shock it has sent reverberating back through his senses. In truth I have conjured this four ball in order to test how well he can maintain a higher vibration in the presence of a lower vibration...and the manner of his behaviour shows that he has some work to do now down this hole.

What I am doing is setting a test that has been set many times before in the ancient cultures. For instance there was once an earnest yogi who disappeared into a mountain cave for months in order to meditate peacefully on compassion and forgiveness...and yet he just exploded when a man turned up and started provoking him with obscenities. This man came as a test to see how far the yogi had come in living his practice...and the situation revealed perfectly that he still had a lot further to go. If we are willing to admit it; difficult people and jarring situations always serve a purpose in revealing back to us where we really are at in our game.

But why does the four ball here represent the lower vibration that has come to jar him off his centre? Well let us remember that he has been accelerating and accelerating through this back nine; whizzing around in his own little introspective bubble and raising his vibrations until in his lightness he has touched the kingdom of heaven deep within. There are simply no resistances left within him. But now he is turning back outwards into the world; smack bang into it in fact.

This is because the four ball ahead are not only four times larger in mass but they are playing a completely different game of golf. They are the ones content with playing a more outwardly sociable form of golf, and though it appears as if both are playing by the same rules, they have not been going through the fire and stripping away all their excess baggage like he has. They are a big heavy blob sitting on the horizon and they serve perfectly as a representation of the current state of humanity in the world whose state of consciousness is not vibrating at a particularly high level. This is not said as a condescending judgment but is merely an observation of the current facts. Take a look around and it's not hard to see that the vast majority of people in this world are living in a three-dimensional paradigm of separation, conflict and competition. In our private meditations we may try and pretend otherwise but in truth this still remains by far the most popular form of golf that people come and play. And he now has to find a way to step back into that world.

But the lives and consciousness of other people are not the matter at hand here. The simple question I am posing here on this sixteenth is whether he is going to be strong enough to hold firm to his integrity in their midst or whether he will be simply pulled down into resonance with their lower collective vibration. Will he be able to abide by the deepest truth that he has only just uncovered in the core of his being?

His rhetorical question gives the immediate answer that he has been affected immediately by the circumstances around him. From playing the game at his own pace and rhythm he is suddenly forced to fall in line with their far slower speed of play and he is forced to wait a good five minutes before they have moved out of range so that he can take his shot. It is in this waiting period that he needs to hold on to his centre without wavering but I can see that impatience has taken a hold over his psyche and that his composure has been shot. The timing of the second shot when he finally played it was then all out of sync. He duffs the shot horribly along the ground and then immediately hangs his head in shame at what he has done.

Afterwards I can see the thought processes tick ticking in his mind as he inevitably starts to project blame upon the lower vibration ahead for pulling him down from the graceful flow he was basking in. Powerlessly he is forgetting to take responsibility for his own game and his energy is starting to drop down in resonance with that of the collective as his thoughts are pulled into a negative place of separation and conflict. For very swiftly there is no longer the room for him to express himself freely and he is competing for, and failing to find, the space *just to be*. The tumbling descent has taken place very quickly from the silent exaltation of the previous hole to now when he is fast losing control of his thoughts. Do I intervene here or give him a chance to rein them back in?

I decide to give him a chance but he is clearly finding it difficult to regain his composure ahead of playing the third shot as he struggles to release what has just taken place and to come back into his centre and into his power. Deep emotions of anger have been triggered towards the group of four ahead who are just innocently going about their game and who know no better than what they are doing. They are completely unaware that there is a fuming solitary player coming up fast behind them who just wants to steamroller his way through and to shake them up along the way!

The group ahead are still just within range and so he has to come to a stop once more and to let the energy of anger simmer inside with no possible outlet of release. All he wants to do is to go ahead and play his shot; but whenever the lives of other people are brought into the equation such a simple act is not always possible to perform. His behaviour is now governed by rules of etiquette that he has no choice but to obey. He looks longingly towards me and towards the wilderness that I am standing in and holds out his arms helplessly at the situation he finds himself in. It is clearly time for me to return again to his side.

'I don't know if all I can do this. How can I possibly keep my cup empty when life is just trying to fill it up with all of this heavy crap?' he asks exasperatedly.

'This is something you have to work through in order to fulfil your vow,' I warn. 'This is so because if everyone in the world was playing the game at your pace everything would be so easy and simple from here on in. But most people are not playing the game at this pace because most people aren't ready to empty their cup. When you first came out on the course you had to separate from them like water from oil because you were not strong enough to go through your training in their presence. But this separation now has to be healed for these are the people you have to return and work with. You have to *be* there to help lead them through the homeward gate.'

'But that's a contradiction! You've just said that most people in my life aren't ready to change so what do you want me to do; bully them into it?'

'Just because they are not ready does not mean they are not

187

willing. Remember that *everyone* has to go through the fire eventually; it is all simply a question of when the timing is ripe. Never judge someone as being too far away from the gate as change can happen in an instant and it can come to a sinner as much as a saint. But at the same time you are not here to try and change or fix anyone for that is simply none of your business.'

'Well if I am not here to change the lives of other people then what is my part to play in their own story of awakening?'

'Your part is simply to give the invitation and to hold the space where transformation can occur. You are to be a channel through which grace can flow subtly to touch the world and its people and to send their lives spinning in new and unplanned directions. The challenge you are facing here on this sixteenth is how well you can maintain that invitation in their company.'

'Well you saw by my second shot that I am not doing much good with that,' he admits honestly.

'You have a lot of anger in you towards this situation you find yourself in. Do not think that this is a bad thing though because that energy is the fuel you need for the task at hand. What you must do is turn that energy from fiery anger into the deepest compassion. That is how you will stop the heavy crap, as you call it, from coming in to fill your cup and that is how you can remain centred and present right here in your power without being affected by what is going on around you. Compassion is your way through this sixteenth hole.'

'So how do I turn my anger into this compassion then?'

'Can you see how a natural pause point has been created in your game by the presence of the group ahead? There are these moments of waiting which are inevitably created in a world that is not yet vibrating at a high enough frequency for life to flow seamlessly and with perfect synchronicity. It is as if the game is being played with the brakes on which inevitably creates this whole congestive stop-start effect. This whole puzzling phenomena has even been discovered by traffic experts investigating congestion on the major highways and who found that when just one person dabs his brakes it can swiftly lead to a massive tailback a few miles back down the road. Let it be said that an ounce of fear, and its massive knock-on consequences, is simply the known way of life in this world at present for many.'

'And so how does knowing all of this help?'

'Well it is these inevitable tailbacks that causes the frustration and anger in this world in people who intuitively know that life could just flow so much more smoothly if we were all to take our foot of the brake. Deep down you know that all human's are loving, generous and kind but fear blinds you from really believing it. Out of that fear many cumbersome things in this world have been created to protect humanity from her own worst excesses rather than helping her fulfil her potential. Without this fear there would be no need for money, war, government's, law, or many other things. Yet you keep all these in place because you wrongly believe that if ever you are going to take the foot off the brake then you will all have to do it together; and of course that moment in history never comes. Instead all you are left with are dreams of a tomorrow that may be less fearful and frustrating than today.

'But in spite of your seeming helplessness to turn things around; in the midst of these congested moments, where there is nowhere to go and nothing to do, you have a choice of where to put your attention and you don't yet realise that this is in itself powerful enough to bring about a revolution. It is in these moments that you would be wise to start practicing compassion for yourself and others around you rather than helplessly perpetuating the cycle of fear and anger. All you have to do is come back to your breathing and send out thoughts of loving kindness. Eventually you may discover that your anger has been transformed and you are right back in your heart centre in a place of deep peace and serenity. Then when the group ahead moves on you will be able to carry on with your game without any fuss or concern. You will find that magically your cup has been emptied and that the game will flow simply again once more.'

'So I just have to see these moments of waiting as another chance to practice?'

'Yes; and then after a while you will no longer even feel the need to label it as a moment of waiting!'

'But are you sure I don't have to do anything else? Don't I have to do more to try and tackle these fears that cause everyone to put the foot on the brake and to stop the flow?'

'At this point in the game you have to take the only responsibility you can which is to make sure that you don't perpetuate the cycle of fear and anger which only causes things to spiral further. Where they arise practice compassion. That truly is the first and wisest response you can do in the situation.'

With that instruction taken to heart he releases me to return back from whence I came and turns his eyes to the group of four ahead. They are still in range of his third shot and so he stands there and turns inwards. I can see that the anger hasn't dissipated with our conversation but it is obvious that there is more spacious detachment from it now than before and he has room to make a wiser choice. His breathing is running deep and true and his heart opens as he begins to send out thoughts of loving kindness to himself and then to them:

May you be well.
May you be happy.
May you be free from suffering.
May you be content and at peace.

Again and again this mantra is repeated until the group have moved away from range and he can safely approach his third shot. I watch on approvingly as I can see that he is standing there far more balanced and poised now than when he approached his second. Grace can return to touch his game and so the rest of the hole pans out without any more undue fuss or concern. When the putt was sunk, a bogey six was recorded on the scorecard, and he is ready to move on to the seventeenth.

The Path of Forgiveness

I have watched in good heart as he went forth alone and completed the 16th hole calmly having rediscovered his patience and poise that had been momentarily lost by the changing circumstances around him. But though it is pleasing to see how swiftly he has taken to heart the practice of compassion, I know that there are still more challenges that lie ahead of him over the remaining two holes of the course.

The 17th is a short 130 yard par three that passes across a narrow stream that runs parallel just ten yards beyond the teeing area. The green beyond is guarded all around on the front three sides by a single deep bunker. It is the shortest hole on the course and the small distance can easily lead to complacency. Believe it or not; many a duff iron has ended up falling into those murky waters from a mindless swing.

He comes to the teeing area and notices that the group ahead are mucking around in search of a stray ball that has become lost in the bushes on the left hand side. Immediately he turns to his practice before any sign of frustration can take hold and for the moment this sustains him well. The minutes pass by and the group seem oblivious to the one who is waiting patiently on the teeing area behind them and so do not wave him to play through. I turn and see approvingly that their noticeable lack of awareness is not ruffling him at all and he is standing there calmly whilst sending out thoughts of loving kindness.

But then something happens that totally cuts right through

this noble practice. It was just a momentary glance; a look back from one of the men playing ahead who suddenly had a flash of awareness that there might be someone nearby watching him. That flash was not the problem; but it was what the man did next that totally threw my student off balance. Actually it was more what the man did not do; as he swiftly turned back around without a word to his companions and just carried on calmly looking for the missing ball. The lone figure on the tee had been rudely snubbed and that in itself was what cut right through.

I turned and saw him shrink back immediately into himself as if a pin had burst his bubble. That one snub had totally deflated his sense of power and authority in the situation and once more he looks across pleadingly in my direction for help. Once more then I must return back to his side.

'Did you see what that guy just did? It's one thing doing this practice when you can think that people just don't know any better than what they are doing; but it is harder to accept when they behave spitefully like that!'

'It's important to stay detached and to not take it so personally,' I warn.

'So you want me to just overlook it and to carry on sending loving thoughts out?'

'I am not saying that at all. The practice isn't to do with sweeping things under the carpet and saying how lovely things are when deep inside you know it is not. To practice compassion you first have to own and honour whatever you are feeling and experiencing; and only then can you go beyond them. So tell me; what is it you are feeling right now?'

'I am still angry I guess,' he answers after a moment's thought.

'Angry about what?'

'Well I guess I expect to be treated better than this.'

'How do you expect to be treated?'

'Well it would be nice to be recognised and for them to understand that I am here to help them if only they would let me.'

'So this goes right back to what you said when you first crossed over these gates and the pain you felt from having to cut your ties with the old world. It goes back to the grief you felt that even though you were trying to make something worthwhile of your life that the people you were close to only turned their back on you. Is this something like you are feeling now with this gentleman ahead?'

'You're probably right. It is tough though isn't it to expect me to do this work with others when I am no longer going to play my part in the tribe.'

'It is very tough indeed,' I concur. 'On the sixteenth there was still quite a bit of distance between you and them for you to quietly go about your practice. Now the whole purpose of this short seventeenth is to see how well you can hold yourself when you are dealing with people in the world when it is more in your face. This is what you are here to learn.'

'Can't I just keep a little bit of distance? I have to say that it is all a bit unsettling and uncomfortable to be so close in their company like this?

'Of course it's uncomfortable! It is very difficult to form relationships with people when you no longer have tribal bonds to help make connections. You are now more socially awkward for you see the world far differently to them. You are an outsider and you do not fit into their box and so they will not make it easy for you to be in their company. From now on it will be a struggle for you to try and find your little niche in the world so that this discomfort will not become too unbearable.'

'But how can they possibly know that I am no longer one of them?' the thought suddenly dawns on him.

'It is because you are standing here alone.'

'Really? What possible difference does that make?'

'As a lone player out here you have little social rank and

influence on this golf course where the rules of etiquette only extend to those who come and play socially in groups of two, three or four. The reason the gentleman ahead didn't let you through is not because of personal spite but because he is simply complying by these social conventions. Do you realise that if you had company you would already have been waved through in an instant? But now you play alone in this world you no longer have a voice to speak up or do anything. No place is set for you at the table and so your challenge here is to try and remember that, though the odds seem stacked against you, worldly power is no real match for the power of spiritual truth that you have come to realise out here. Though in their company you seem weak you must uphold your conviction that coming out here with me was right.'

'It's no wonder I feel like I am grieving! Being so close like this reminds me of my old life when I fitted in so easily and comfortably with other people. I crave their company and to just be someone who has a place set at the table for them. It is so tempting to doubt that this really is right; standing here alone and so uncomfortable like this I mean.'

'But were you truly happy squishing into shoes that never perfectly suited you? Can you not remember the discontent you felt that first caused you to walk through those gates and into my hands?'

'Yes, deep down I do know that my memories are becoming selective and that this is all just another test of my faith,' he admits sadly. 'But it is still a temptation to try and claw back my worldly powers again; to fit in again.'

'I understand that perfectly and you are not alone in your struggle for what you are experiencing now is exactly what all contemplatives have experienced through the ages. It is slightly different in eastern cultures, but here in the west, the lone player in golf and in life has always been the messenger bringing a message that the world doesn't wish to hear. Not only did they close their ears to it; throughout your history that messenger has all too often been persecuted and killed for it. The lone golfer is misunderstood and mistrusted in a society whose rules have never served to accommodate them. And though your world is mainly tolerant when these contemplatives retreat into the confined cloisters of the monastery and go about their business safely away from view…it creates a lot of problems for them when that contemplative dares to venture out onto the course; and to even come and play on the same hole as them.'

'But why does it create so many problems for them?'

'Why do you think? You know already that the contemplative carries with him a precious truth that has the power to shake the very foundations upon which they live. By the very nature of his *being*, the contemplative quietly questions all social norms and ways of living. So that is why the golfing fraternity has a long held and deeply ingrained wariness about the lone golfer who dares to venture out onto the course and who doesn't stay put on the practice ground or on the range where he is meant to be. If golf is set up as a social sport where we fill in the spaciousness of the golf course with mind games of competitive scoring along with social chit chat and completion of business deals…then what does this lone golfer *do* in the intervals between striking his ball?

'This is the one question that few golfers would wish to consider answering because they are so uncomfortable with the contemplative who dares to use this silent, spacious, eternal moment to go within himself when they have spent the best part of their lives running away from themselves.'

'It's truly amazing to think that just by me *being* here that all of this is going on underneath the surface.'

'That's exactly the point. You are not meant to say or do anything to provoke a reaction. Just be the presence here and don't get drawn into a chain reaction where you start to behave as they would like you to.'

'How would they like me to behave here though?'

'Powerlessly. They need to try and convince themselves that playing out here alone is a sign of weakness not strength. This is why they are unconsciously trying to undermine you. You must show them otherwise?'

'It's a bit ironic that this is all being disguised as polite social etiquette,' he says dryly. 'The only question is how to show them.'

'As I've already said you must start by feeling fully into the hurt you are experiencing right now and face it fearlessly without blinking. Then you must let it all go by giving your forgiveness to all that created this hurt. Having a little more understanding of what is really going on behind that man's snub can help make it easier to practice this forgiveness. For instance, can you understand that though his eyes appeared aware of your presence; there is a bigger part of him that did not even see you at all? It is through this process of forgiveness that you will be able to stay detached in these situations and to stay centred in your power. '

'Is that all?'

'It may sound simple but when you put it into practice you will see it is the hardest thing a human being can do. For centuries now we have been practicing the opposite. Rather than facing this hurt we avoid it in all our defensive ways and project blame onto others. And rather than forgiving and letting go this hurt we hold on and perpetuate it with our identification with it.'

'But how will going beyond this habit of defensiveness help?'

'It will heal the separation that exists between you and the group of four men ahead at present. Ideally you want to hold back and wait for them to make the first move by gesturing you to play the shot. You want them to offer their hand of forgiveness because you think they are the ones who have the power to do so. This is what you are doing and in the meantime the separation remains and builds. But you are the one with the power and it is up to you now to make peace in your own heart by forgiving and letting go. Then you will be amazed by what can happen.'

'But how does forgiveness help me to use my power wisely?'

'If you react by escaping the hurt in whatever strategy you choose; you will give away your power and your presence. You will be playing the games of separation, competition, and conflict on their terms and will not be maintaining a higher truth on my terms. The last hole was a lesson to help put that boundary of integrity in place. Now you must go further and hold that line. Do not budge. Do not compromise. Stand tall. And do all of this not with the intent of conquering and not with the attitude of 'my terms are better than your terms' but with the genuine desire to bring about unity and peace. It is time for you to stand up and to end the war. Can you do that for me?'

'I can,' he finally answers after a long, long moment of reflective silence. 'But I don't see how it will change anything between me and them?' he adds.

'Don't be so defeatist! If you don't behave as they wish you to behave you may be surprised by what can happen next.'

He falls quiet and softly withdraws into himself in order to seek the jewel of forgiveness inside.

'Okay I can feel my heart getting warmer and I no longer feel the rejection as strongly as I once did. I have some perspective on what it is about now. I don't blame them for snubbing me. I know what it is like to be in their shoes.'

After going through this short and sweet time of reflection I gently point ahead and lift his eyes to what is now taking place.

'See what can happen. They are now calling you to play your shot!'

'Really,' he responds astonished by the sudden transformation from an atmosphere of hostility towards one of friendliness. 'I did all that just by changing my perspective?' he adds holding up his arm in acknowledgment of their gesture.

'When you honour the highest truth in yourself you are also inviting them to honour it in themselves too. This can swiftly pull you both out of the old tribal mentality into a place of mutual communion. It can pull down these false barriers of insider/outsider and suddenly for the first time they can really see you standing here. Regardless of these hostile social conventions on the surface;

in seeing you it is simply human nature to act kindly.'

He walks over to his bag and begins to mull over which club to take. As he does so I can see some agitation take hold as if feeling under pressure to get on with things. No matter that he has been kept waiting here for many minutes; he clearly doesn't wish to destroy the peace by disrupting their game too much in return.

'You must continue to stay firm in your power in the shot you play,' I warn. 'As you are socially inferior in their company, I know it is tempting for you to rush the shot to get out of their way quick or to play the percentages by playing a more contained and controlled shot. But you must resist this temptation and must play the shot as if they were not their watching and to commit to it fully. You must take the risk and go all out on it without any fear. You must now stand tall and stay visible before the eyes of the world.'

He listens without a further word. Giving a gentle nod of his head he lets go of the eight iron that he was about to take hold of; and pulls out the nine instead. Turning within, he begins to put absolutely everything into the shot at hand by draining his cup as much as he can. Past and future; here and there – these have all disappeared from his mind as he has gone smoothly into that eternal moment where all is possible. He is ready to play the shot, and bang, the nine iron flies through to strike the ball ever so crisply towards the target. It is so sweetly struck that the ball stops virtually dead on landing; finishing about ten feet wide of the flag. To my watching eye it is as if the ball has fallen softly into the lap of God. Ooh it has given me goose bumps to see the way the ball surrendered itself into the green's cushioned surface so quietly and so serenely.

Calmly he picks up the bag and walks on over the little bridge towards the green. Not one hurried step is taken and I watch approvingly to see that he is now radiating such confidence and presence. Regardless of popular opinion; he knows now without a shadow of doubt exactly who he is and he also knows for certain that worldly powers could never ever fill his cup like it has just been filled. He wants for nothing and so it is that in this peaceful state he

199

gives a warm gesturing hand of acknowledgment to the four men. I can see that they are standing around and looking bedazzled by this illumined solitary figure in their midst and who is simply oozing with charisma. The subtle power play that had been taking place between them and him only a few moments ago was simply blown away to nothing.

He drops the bag gracefully down to the floor and takes the putter in hand whilst one of the men kindly pulls out the flag from the hole. Again the temptation is there to rush the shot and to move on swiftly through to the last. The temptation is there to shrink and to not impose his presence upon their game in any way. But he is now very mindful of this and so will not be as easily agitated off his centre. He takes a step back to gather himself; before moving in and sinking that ten foot putt for his second birdie. In doing so I am left without any doubt that he has truly passed the test of this seventeenth hole. Keenly then he is ready to move on towards the eighteenth and final hole of this particular game.

A Bottomless Compassion for the World

He has come to the eighteenth tee; but I can see that he is not standing here looking ahead in confident celebration at how far he has come and to a minor milestone that he is close to reaching. He is hesitating because he is looking back at the group of four men who are now putting out on the seventeenth green and who he longs to accompany up this last. Could he not break the rules by inviting them to join him up this final hole as a group of five? Could he not finish the game with them by his side?

These are all questions from a self who is trying to wrap up the game neatly on his terms. He may not see it, but part of his desire to join forces with these men is so that he can teach them his ways and so that they may end up honouring him as their guru, saviour or whatever else he may long to call to himself. It is time for me to return to his side once more then before these dreamy ideas run amok.

'Grace is a subtle force my friend. It comes and touches those who cross its path but then just as swiftly it moves on. Always remember to keep the cup empty. You must let them go and let them be.'

'But there is so much more I could do here with them,' he answers longingly. 'With this power that has been unleashed in me I could rewrite the whole rulebook of social convention and I could usher them into this brave new world that you have shown to me. I cannot help but worry that I haven't touched them enough to have made any difference to the way they play the game.'

'How they play the game is none of your business and you must remember that the power within you is not yours to possess and wield at your own will. You are but a channel and your only responsibility is to keep your cup empty and to play your own game. You must trust that this is enough of a life for you to lead.'

'But that seems a terribly lonely life does it not! There is so much that could be done to make this world a friendlier place, a more inviting and welcoming place, for those who come out here and play the game alone. Isn't this the ending we are trying to create here?'

'This is all just your mind trying to claim the prize from your mission for itself. But we have come to the point in the game where I have to tell you that there is no prize; there is no pot of gold at the end of the rainbow. This is simply the part you have to play and you will have to play that part until the game is done. Stop trying to be the hero here and move on.'

'That all sounds incredibly cold and harsh,' he protests defensively. 'So I am just meant to go around and around this course until the siren sounds to end the game?'

'It's not quite like that. You won't have to go around and around *this* particular course; just the course of life! It sounds depressing but if you live fully in the moment such thoughts will never have need to touch you. All the while your only guiding intention is to keep your cup empty and to let grace move you through your life as best you can. You must go ahead and play your shots and to cross paths with whomsoever you are meant to cross paths with. Sometimes those paths will join together for a while and sometimes they will just intersect for the briefest of moments. Regardless of the situation the instruction of just carrying on to play your game remains the same. In the end nothing else matters but that and whether you think you made a difference or not is completely irrelevant in the grand scheme of things. Remember all of this is very humble work you are doing here.'

'But do you not think that this humbling work is a very tough assignment?'

'It is the toughest,' I answer agreeably. 'Let me take you back to the moment when you first crossed those gates. Turning back around would have been an easy assignment. Or let me take you back to the first green when life seemed so fresh and magical. Staying here would also have been an easy assignment. Or what about the fifteenth hole where you played so freely with the jewel of self realisation in your hand. Time and space were irrelevant in that moment and you were quite happy just to be in this eternal place. Finishing here also would have been the easiest assignment. But you have kept on going because you know that there is a deep schism that runs between my world and yours and that this schism has to be healed. So rather than taking the easy way you have kept on going because you know you are only here to fulfil your vow and to do the real work of bridging that gap between heaven and earth.

Now, the only place where this work can be done is in the desolate frontier between these two worlds. No-one lives here and there is no obvious sustenance to be found anywhere. It is a hard place to be and all of our training together on this golf course has been to prepare you with the courage to live in this place and to not escape from it in fear. Not many have that courage for the temptation is strong to either retreat back fully into the kingdom of heaven or to fall with both feet back into the kingdom of earth. Sometimes it is just a temporary lapse; often it is more lasting. And the only reason that people lapse is not because it is impossible to be here but because they forget the one thing that can sustain their presence here. But you don't need me to tell you at the moment what that one thing is. You know well enough now what fills your cup to the brim. Yet despite this knowing; your struggle is that you still hope that one day this barren land will turn itself into a golden oasis and that you won't have to depend solely on this one mysterious and unknown source of sustenance that you cannot control the supply of and which constantly leaves your nerves wracked as to whether it will come again. Your deepest fear is not that you will forget...but that one day you will empty the cup and it won't be filled again.'

'Wow that's sure a lot of stuff to try and take in,' he answers with a blowing puff of his cheeks. 'So you think I want to change the world here not to help everyone else but simply because I want to turn this desert into an oasis for myself? Man that's a heavy charge to lay at my door!'

'It is a natural hope to have; the hope that being in this betwixt and between place is only a temporary affair and not something a little more long lasting. It is a real test of resolve to go through with this when there is no sight of an ending.'

'So will this desert ever become an oasis?'

'Never. It will always remain a place suited for transition rather than a paradise suited for settling down; a place where souls come to pass through from one state of being to another. And not only will you have to remain in this desolate place for a while; but you will have to be here until every other living soul has passed through the gate into the kingdom of heaven. In addition you will also have to be here in the knowledge that there is nothing you can do to even try and speed up that whole process. Only when all that is complete will the siren sound for you to come back home.'

'Are you really sure I agreed to this back up their in the stars where I came down from? If I did then I can't believe I quite knew what on earth I was signing up for. You really want me to stand here without any power or control over when I can leave?'

'That's right. Just keep emptying your cup, play your shots, and then let grace take care of the rest.'

'You make it all sound so simple,' he responds with a wry shake of his head. Even though he finds it hard to believe at the moment I can see that deep within he knows all the same that thy will must be done. His compassion for the world is simply too strong to resist.

He pulls out the driver from his bag and looks ahead to a long and tricky par four that has been designed as a final test for the weary golfer who has come this far. There are mature trees lining the left side of a narrow fairway which then turns sharply to the right and opens out to reveal a small green guarded by several deep bunkers. The driveway runs alongside the right hand side of this hole and many a stray ball has crossed out of bounds from the teeing area. As he places the ball on the tee peg I can see one final question looming at the forefront of his mind.

'Am I alone doing this work or are there other souls out there fulfilling this same vow too?'

'Trust me when I say that you are not alone out here and many have completed or are going through this same journey as you already. Some go on to work together in small groups. Some work together in large New-Age communities. Others quietly work alone beneath the radar doing the same job they did before. Some are working as worldbridgers in very obvious ways; many are doing this very subtly. I cannot tell you what your way in the outside world will be; I cannot tell you whether you will join a like-minded group or whether you will work alone. I cannot tell you where your life will be guided. All you can do is follow your heart and allow life to guide you along your path. As I said; sometimes you will cross paths with someone and join for a while whilst other times your paths will just intersect. Don't think or worry about this too much.

My only final word of warning is to be aware of wolves parading in sheep's clothing. It is easy in some cases to know when you are selling your soul but sometimes you will cross paths with well intentioned souls who speak the right language and who will try and persuade you that they can give you sustenance. The desert is a hard and lonely place to be and you will seem vulnerable pray to those who seek your allegiance. Because of this the marketplace is simply jammed full of self help manuals and workshops offered by those who think they have the answers. Be not cynical about these offerings but simply stay strong in your centre and in what you know is true for you. Remember that at the end of the day all the answers you need lie within you. '

'So are all of these well-intentioned helpers never to be heeded? Am I never to give my trust to another living soul?'

'I am not saying that at all. You need to stay open when

someone crosses your path and some will indeed come to help point you towards the truth within just as much as others will come to obscure it. You just need to be aware and vigilant at all times and you must make sure that the only source of sustenance you are drawing upon is the same as what you are drawing upon now. If ever you find yourself relying on another source to fill your cup; then that is a sure sign that it is time for you to move on. As I say the easy opt-outs are always tempting you to forget what it is that truly sustains you. Maintaining your connection to the sacred is something that will really require your constant attention.'

'It all sounds like a bit of a minefield out there,' he answers warily as he suddenly looks ahead towards the challenging eighteenth hole before him.

'Do not be afraid. With your training behind you, and with enough experience, it is not too hard to spot when you are falling off the path. And remember; if ever you falter the golf course and I will always be here to put you right again. Know that there is no place out here or in the world where you can fall so far so as to not be reached.'

With these instructions taken to heart he quietly and steadily plays his way up the last. Like the fifteenth there isn't a lot to tell about what takes place in the interval between here and there. All that is left to say is that when he came to the eighteenth green he was standing over a long twelve foot putt for par. Long shadows from the looming clubhouse have cast themselves across the green and everything has fallen silent in anticipation whilst he hovers over the shot ahead. Without fuss the putt is directed smoothly into the cup; but there is none of the fist pumping that marked the end of the first half of his game. Instead all he uttered was a quiet thank you to the heavens for this sweet ending to his game.

As he placed the flag back into the cup and hands me back my set of clubs, there is no celebratory sense of completion and he doesn't dare to try and shake my hand again. He knows as well as I that the work has only just begun.

Thank you for your purchase of this book.

Author's rely heavily on customer feedback for marketing and promotion of their work. You are warmly encouraged, therefore, to provide a review on the sales channel for this book; on the Amazon website.

About the Author

R.A. Moseley is an English writer currently living in Margaret River, in the South-West corner of Australia, with his wife Melissa and his cat Grace.

His mission in life is to be a spiritual friend; one who uses the power of the written word to illuminate that there is far more going on beneath the surface of our day-to-day human existence.

The Kingdom of Golf is Within You is the third of four publications to his name. Other titles are:

The Search for Satya (2012)

Tracking Fritz's Footsteps: Meditations on E.F. Schumacher's A Guide for the Perplexed (2013)

and

Hamartia (2018)

All titles are self-published through Create Space; with print and e-book copies available for purchase through Amazon and other online distributors.

www.ingramcontent.com/pod-product-compliance
Lightning Source LLC
Chambersburg PA
CBHW031837090426
42741CB00005B/269